FORESTOPIA

FORESTOPIA
A PRACTICAL GUIDE TO
THE NEW FOREST ECONOMY

By Michael M'Gonigle and Ben Parfitt

Alan Etkin, Project Co-ordinator

Harbour Publishing

Published by
HARBOUR PUBLISHING
P.O. Box 219
Madeira Park, BC Canada V0N 2H0

Published with the assistance of the Canada Council and the Government of British Columbia, Cultural Services Branch

Cover, page design and composition by Roger Handling, Glassford Design
Cover photograph by Garth Lenz
Author photograph by Alan Etkin
Printed and bound in Canada

Canadian Cataloguing in Publication Data
M'Gonigle, R. Michael.
Forestopia

Includes bibliographical references and index.
ISBN 1-55017-096-1

1. Forests and forestry – British Columbia – Economic aspects. 2. Forest management – British Columbia. I. Parfitt, Ben. II. Forestopia Project. III. Title.
SD568.B7M56 1994   333.75'09711 C94-910170-2

Forestopia began as a research project by the graduate research seminar of Simon Fraser University's School of Resource and Environmental Management. Later, in the spring of 1993, four graduate students—Bryan Evans, Lee Montgomery, Murray Rutherford and Sue Todd—researched some of the themes addressed in the book before gathering with the authors at a work retreat at Lasqueti Island in the early summer of 1993. Bryan Evans later took on the difficult task of gathering and researching most of the sources that yielded the boxed quotes and excerpts sprinkled throughout this text. Bryan always knew where the sources were, a not inconsiderable task. To Bryan for his insightful criticisms of the text in early draft stages and for his unfailing ability to access the right information, we owe our thanks.

Major funding for this project was provided by BC Wild–Earthlife Canada, the Bullitt Foundation of Seattle and VanCity Credit Union. Supporters of Greenpeace also gave assistance as did over 300 individual donors, some of whose names appear on page 6. The generosity of all is gratefully acknowledged. Much of the research and writing was undertaken under the auspices of the Institute for New Economics, and we wish to thank Edith Davidson for her continuing work on the Institute's behalf.

Early drafts were reviewed by Jim Cooperman, Ken Drushka, Ray Travers and Howard White of Harbour Publishing. Their comments and criticisms were invaluable. The major textual edit was undertaken by Mary Schendlinger whose thoughtful work and patience helped make this book a better product. To all who read the text and offered advice, our thanks. Roger Handling undertook the challenge of creating an effective design for the book, to the specifications of authors, project co-ordinator and publisher.

To Alan Etkin we owe our greatest debt. He co-ordinated all aspects of the project. From fundraising efforts, to last-minute photography, to canvassing the province for the pictures spread through the text, to formatting text so that two computer illiterates could read each other's copy, to storing copy and sources in readily accessible files, we owe our heartfelt appreciation. Collaborations are difficult things, more so when you're the last link in the chain. Alan had the dubious distinction of being that link, having to wait as we pushed deadlines back or made text changes that affected the placement of graphics in the book. Without his extraordinary patience and good humour through most of that process, this book would not have been possible.

Finally, a short but warm word of thanks to Fabienne Goulet, Alicia Priest and Wendy Wickwire who are all by now a trifle leery of that oft-repeated phrase: "This is the last thing left to do." To them, the authors and project co-ordinator continue to be most indebted.

Everyone involved in the Forestopia Project is grateful to the following people,
whose generosity made the development of this book possible.

Louise S. Alden & Edward H. Alden
Frederic Back
Arnold Baker
Cristina Baldazzi
Steven Barer & Susan Albersheim
Steve & Linda Barnard
Tom & Kerry Barnhardt
B. J. Benson
John B. Benson
Don & Gisele Bentley
David Beringer & Rachel Leigh
Elisabeth Bosher
Dr. V. Warren Bourgeois
G. Brewster
Andrew & Helen Brink
Chuck Brody
Bob Browning
Melda Buchanan
Michael Chechik
Vivian J. Chenard
Vi Chungranes
Rod & Francie Church
Russel & Joyce Clark
W. John Clark
L. F. Cohen
W. R. & P. N. Collinson
Frances E. Compston
E. Mary Craig
Mrs. Lois Dallamore
Alice Davies
Dr. Allan J. Davies
Mike Day
Anne de Cosson
M. Devine
Eberhard & Sarah Diehl
Lawrence M. Dill
Graham Dowden
Alan Drengson and Victoria Stevens
Robert Drislane
Frank R. Dubery
Luc Duchesne
Dr. Allen C. Eaves & Family
Leonor Etkin
Joseph G. Exner
James Farnham Dew
David & Marnie Fisher
Nadine Fletcher
Catrina Fortune
Eric Fraikin
Jess Franks
Lloyd A. Fraser
Mark E. Gabas
Susan Gage
Sonia and Angus Galbraith
Kenneth A. Gamey
John R. Gellard
Pedro & Luce Georlette
Len Gilday
Mary Gradnitzer
Doug Graeb & Joan Frost
Laura Graves
Wayne & Anita Gray
Alanda Greene
Charles Greene

W. Greensides
Philip Haddad
Dr. Jack C. Hallam
E. Hannah
Margaret L. Hartt
John Haydn
Phil Hein
H. Albert Hestler
Perry & Audrey Hnetka
Eric & Inge Hohndorf
Susan Holvenstot
Paul L. Hunter
Eveline Inksetter
Intevec Forestry Consulting—
    Garth & Kathleen
Alan C. James
Lynne Jamieson & Paul Pasternak
Stuart Jamieson
Susan Joiner & William O. Gilsdorf
Martin & Esther Kafer
Jo Kehoe
Duncan Kippan
Kris Klaasen & Joni Miller—
    Working Design
Shirley Kricheldorf
Aline La Flamme
Zoe Laird
Claude P. Leger
Camille Lindseth
Donald A. L. Macintyre
Ian Mackenzie
Celeste MacLeod
Andrew Macwatt
Eleanor Mae
Timo Makinen
Tara G. Martin
Patrick W. Matakala
James A. McLean
Bessie L. McMurray
Ken Melamed & Ursula Scherer
Peggie Merlin
Glenda Miller
Alex and Ruth Moffoot
Tom Mommsen
Doug Morton
Kevin Murphy
Peter J. Murphy
Carol Murray
M. R. Mussar
Lasha G. Nault
Dr. David B. Nerman
Bruce Newmarch
William Niemann
Lynne Nilsson
Don Olds
In loving memory of Fraeda Olenick
Stan Olson
Rick O'Neill
Michael & Bodil Oppenheimer
Joan & Bill Paterson
Tony D. Pearse
Norman, Imke & Tanya Pearson
E. & M. Pechlaner
Lloyd C. Peterson

Bill Pike
Ruth Powell
Peter Puhakka Jr.
Wendell M. Ratcliffe &
    Marjorie Young
I. Raudzins
Eugene & Carole Reiner
Howard Rice
W. G. Richardson
Helmut Rietzler, Dipl. Ing.
Kim C. Roberts
Ed Rooney
Martin Rossander
Catherine & Ben Rostron
Peter Rowlands
Craig Runyan
Paul Sanborn
Lothar Schaefer
Jill Schroder
Joan, Nelson & Alan Scott
Deb and Bob Sherwood
Ernest Sieber
Maureen & Tony Simmonds
W. David Sims
Bud Skinner
Peter C. Sleik
Helen W. Sonthoff
Specialized Care Resources
David & Margaret Spencer
Mildred W. Spencer
Dorothy & George Stevens
George Sutherland
Dr. R. Sutherland
Martha Szilagya
Don Tait
Eva F. Temmel
Marco Terwiel
Carol T. Thommasen
David & Lois Thompson
Norman Todd
Dr. Seymour Trieger, Director,
    All About US CANADA
    Foundation
Cathy Turner
J. S. Tyhurst
Wayne Daniel Veldhuis
Sylvia Verity
Stephen Vida
B. & V. Vitols
Cordula Vogt
Angela Wallace
Bernard & Jean Webber
Robert B. H. Welsh
George West
Judy Whitaker
Dr. K. J. Williams
P. Williams
Paul & Ena Wilson
Wayne A. Wolfe
Brian J. Wood
Bruce & Sylvia Woodsworth
Tom & Irene Wright
Nachiko Yokota
Fred C. Zwickel

Chapter 1	Against the Wall	9
Chapter 2	March of the Feller Buncher	19
Chapter 3	Death of a Forest	29
Chapter 4	Economic Surrender	39
Chapter 5	The New Forest Economy	51
Chapter 6	A Business of Stewardship	59
Chapter 7	Financing the Transition	71
Chapter 8	Creating Value	83
Chapter 9	A New Industrial Strategy	95
Chapter 10	Reinventing BC	107
Sources		111
Index		116

AGAINST THE WALL

IN THE SPRING AND SUMMER OF 1993 MORE THAN 800 PEOPLE were arrested on a logging road in one of the most emotionally charged series of demonstrations ever staged in British Columbia. Day after day, the bodies of limp protesters were hauled off by police constables to waiting paddy wagons for the short drive to Ucluelet, a small village on Vancouver Island's southwest coast. There, dozens, sometimes hundreds, of people were charged daily with disobeying a court order preventing them from blockading logging trucks entering the ancient forests of Clayoquot Sound. And as the weeks turned into months, the eyes of the world began to focus on the last large, mostly pristine, temperate rain forest left on southern Vancouver Island.

Almost a year later, on the first day of spring, 1994, British Columbians witnessed a new type of demonstration as an estimated 15,000 forest industry workers and their families descended on Victoria in the biggest mass rally ever staged in front of the provincial legislature. A banner pleading for the government to "listen to the people" was strung between two cranes sitting on log barges in the nearby inner harbour. Standing on the top step of the legislature before the crowd, an obviously troubled Premier Mike Harcourt looked on. Moments before stepping to the podium where he would be drowned out in a roar of boos, the Premier turned to members of the media surrounding him and said: "These are my friends....These are British Columbians concerned about their communities....These are legitimate concerns and we're going to address them. In the past, there have been cases where they've been sacrificed."

As impressive as the crowd's size was that sunny March morning, it was nothing compared to the 24,000-plus workers who had lost their jobs in British Columbia's forest industry the previous decade. One of them, Hank Bonthuis, is a laid-off plywood mill employee. On the day of the mass rally, Bonthuis sat in his Parksville home, content to learn about the day's events in Victoria on the evening news. It was now nearly four years since Bonthuis and more than 300 others had lost their jobs at the plywood mill in nearby Port Alberni. Like many others, Bonthuis can vividly remember the day he started work at "the plywoods." It was July 6, 1956, and the forest-based economy of Vancouver Island was booming. Towns like Port Alberni employed a thousand people and more in individual mills, and the work was easy to come by. At the plywood mill Bonthuis, a seventeen-year-old high school dropout, quickly found work on the bundling line where plywood sheets were wrapped together in kraft paper. "I was

Opposite: The last of Vancouver's ancient rain forest? Old-growth wall mural by Robert Dobie and Terry Gilecki. Ron Woodward photo.

living the good life, making good money," Bonthuis recalls. "I remember the 1960s driving around in a car, and no matter where you drove there was wood. There was trees. In those days it looked like a never ending resource. It looked like there never would be an end."

But then Bonthuis's employer, MacMillan Bloedel Ltd., made a big capital investment in the mill and suddenly it seemed as if no jobs were safe. "We had a mega layoff in the '80s," Bonthuis said. "They added a lot of automated equipment and what it meant was a mill that once carried 912 people then carried 365." Those layoffs and others opened Bonthuis's eyes. "Probably in my forties I really started becoming aware of the diminishing forests, the poor logging practices. You didn't need to go very far to find tonnes of wood lying rotting in the forest."

Since he was laid off for good in 1991, Bonthuis has watched as those remaining in the industry cling to a precarious dependence. For thirty-five years he made good money working for the biggest forest company in the province, and he more than sympathizes with the many industry workers who fear new park proposals. But, he adds, "I see the protesters as being misguided in a sense. They're misguided because eventually there will not be enough trees left to sustain the industry at this level. So you have to make some decisions. Do you stay at this level until it's all run out? Or do we downscale and look for other things, so that maybe our children have some work as well?"

Today, sawmill closures are an almost daily fact of life. Thousands of workers in the woods and mills face the certain loss of high-paying union jobs, and the prognosis is not good. "Some of the communities that I see up in the north here...the Houstons and the Telkwas, these communities are a wisp away from dying," says Mike Tarr, president of Kaien Consumers Credit Union in Prince Rupert. "I think we're going to see more and more of that sort of thing, simply because the economic choices that were made twenty-five, thirty years ago have run their course and we need to replace those with something else."

In BC the forest industry is dominated by volume-oriented mass producers of standard grade or commodity lumber and pulp. For the workers who still have jobs in those industries, there seemingly is no option. Their jobs with the big companies depend on pulling the maximum number of trees out of the forest, then running them through the mills as quickly and "efficiently" as possible. Told this over and over again by their employers, union leaders, even their elected MLAs and MPs, many loggers and mill workers remain convinced that the volume can and must be maintained, that the biggest threat to their livelihood is the environmentalist blockading the logging road—someone like Sile Simpson, a bed and breakfast manager in Tofino.

Twice hauled before the courts for blockading logging roads leading into the temperate rain forests of Clayoquot Sound, Simpson knew the consequences of confronting multinational forest companies as she stood, once again, on a logging road near Tofino in the spring of 1993. Several months earlier a BC Supreme Court Justice had ordered her to "keep the peace." And while the protest she was about to engage in was nonviolent, it violated the judge's order.

Lessons from history

It is more appropriate to think of resources as managing humans than the converse: the larger and the more immediate are prospects for gain, the greater the political power that is used to facilitate unlimited exploitation....Where large and immediate gains are in prospect, politicians and governments tend to ally themselves with special interest groups in order to facilitate the exploitation. Forests throughout the world have been destroyed by wasteful and short sighted forest practices....

Scientists have been active in pointing out environmental degradation and consequent hazards to human life, and possibly to life as we know it on Earth. But by and large the scientific community has helped to perpetuate the illusion of sustainable development through scientific and technological progress. Resource problems are not really environmental problems: they are human problems that we have created at many times and in many places, under a variety of political, social, and economic systems.

Donald Ludwig, Ray Hilborn and Carl Walters, "Uncertainty, Resource Exploitation, and Conservation: Lessons from History," in *Science* (No. 260, 1993).

"I knew I was going for the high jump," Simpson says. "I knew that. And it's interesting. I called the spirit of the bear. And when the police arrested me the bear came. She came from under Kennedy Bridge swimming, looking directly at me." That vision provided sustenance to Simpson for, unlike three others arrested that morning, she went directly to jail for violating the terms of the earlier court order. Not long after, she was sentenced to a six-month prison term and taken to jail in Burnaby. Her sentence was later relaxed, allowing her to become a home prisoner, her movements electronically monitored through a bracelet secured to her ankle.

A lone survivor in Houston Forest Products' clearcut on the north side of Tahtsa Reach. Will Koop photo.

The layoff of Bonthuis and thousands of others in the 1980s and early 1990s went virtually unnoticed, but the protests of Simpson and others resounded around the world. On one day in August 1993, 242 protesters were hauled to jail from Clayoquot Sound. "This will probably be the largest number arrested at any protest I've been involved in," commented RCMP St. Sgt. Len Doyle. "We had seventy-five on Lyell Island with the Haidas. I think the Clayoquot numbers show they're canvassing support around the province, all around North America really. We've arrested people from European countries, the United States and eastern Canada."

Miles away over mountainous watersheds in Port Alberni, mill worker Mark Brett served a quieter and quite different sentence from Simpson, a sentence of uncertainty. Brett is a forty-three-year-old labourer at MacMillan Bloedel Ltd.'s Alberni Pacific Division sawmill, a mill consuming some of the trees falling to chain saws in Clayoquot Sound. Three years earlier, Brett, like Bonthuis, lost a job he'd held for nineteen years at MacMillan Bloedel's plywood mill on the banks of Alberni Inlet. The company closed the mill, eliminating 360 high-paying jobs. Much of the mill's machinery then sold to another MB mill in Pine Hill Alabama where workers earned a third the union rate in Port Alberni.

Brett left high school in grade 10, and eventually followed his father into the plywood mill. Now, long on experience but short on education, he can only watch as jobs disappear in Port Alberni's once booming forest industry and wonder when his turn might come. "I'm working pretty steady right now," Brett says. "But that could change. And it has changed before. There is an indication that they're going to lay some guys off. I'd be with some of the guys to go if that happened. It doesn't look good."

Consuming the capital

Clearly, any human activity dependent on the consumptive use of ecological resources (forestry, fisheries, agriculture, waste disposal, urban sprawl onto agricultural land) cannot be sustained indefinitely if it uses not only the annual production of the biosphere (the "interest") but also cuts into the standing stock (the "capital"). Herein lies the essence of our environmental crisis....

Throughout the industrial revolution we have been busily converting ecological capital into economic capital. In short, the global economy is cannibalizing the biosphere.

William E. Rees, "The Ecology of Sustainable Development," in *The Ecologist* (Vol. 20, No. 1, 1990).

The conflict that surrounds us

Bonthuis, Simpson, Brett—laid-off worker, environmentalist and mill employee—are three individuals involved in an ever-growing conflict that is our daily fare. It is a difficult conflict because it pits against each other two things, both of which we depend on: our economy and our environment. The recession appears to be over, but more and more mill workers face the certain loss of high-paying jobs. At the same time, environmental grievances remain unresolved as old-growth forests become rarer every day. The struggle to preserve the last remaining places left widens, focussing global attention on BC's ancient forests.

Loggers who got themselves arrested, an unusual demonstration at Clayoquot Sound, summer 1993. Josh Berson photo.

On the international front, environmental groups such as Greenpeace wage high-profile campaigns to inform major European buyers of BC pulp and lumber products, about the implications of their purchasing decisions. Premier Harcourt and an entourage of government and forest industry representatives jet to Germany to denounce the so-called "misinformation campaign," which they later blame for the cancellation of two pulp purchasing contracts between British buyers and MacMillan Bloedel Ltd.

Meanwhile, at home, reasoned attempts to quell the conflict have failed. The Commission on Resources and Environment (CORE), a government-appointed commission charged with developing a consensus-based land use plan for Vancouver Island, recently released its long-awaited report, in which it called for a nominal increase in protected areas on the heavily logged island to a total of 13 percent. The recommendations were quickly criticized by environmentalists who had lobbied for 18 percent protection, but even the lesser level triggered outrage among thousands of loggers and mill workers in communities up and down the island. Town halls were packed to overflowing with forest industry workers. Streets were jammed with logging trucks whose drivers leaned heavily on their horns. All demanded Harcourt fire CORE Commissioner Stephen Owen and protect workers' jobs—demands that culminated in the huge Victoria rally.

But even before the protests, many in the environmental and labour communities were cynical when CORE began its deliberations. Given the history of forestry battles in the province, the backlash to the CORE report was entirely to be expected. Indeed, a year earlier when the Harcourt government had first announced its land use plan for Clayoquot—a plan calling for the preservation of

Two forest paradoxes

...hunter gatherers live *in* the forest, agriculturists live *adjacent* to but within striking distance of the forest, and urban-industrial men live *away* from the forest. Paradoxically, the more the spatial separation from the forest, the greater the impact on its ecology, and the further removed the actors from the consequences of this impact!

...the faster the development of formal scientific knowledge about the composition and functioning of forests types, the faster the rate of deforestation...the belief that science provides an infallible guide has nonetheless encouraged major interventions in natural ecosystems, and these have had unanticipated and usually unfortunate consequences. The history of both fisheries and forest management are replete with illustrations of the failure of sustained-yield methods to forestall ecological collapse.

M. Gadgil and R. Guha, *This Fissured Land: An Ecological History of India* (Berkeley CA: University of California Press, 1992).

a third of the region's forests with light to heavy industrial forestry in the other two-thirds—the Premier was emphatic about his government's approach to resolving such disputes. "We've rejected the extreme views of those who say 'Preserve it all' or 'Log it all'," Harcourt said of the so-called Clayoquot compromise. "It was a balanced decision."

Balanced for some, perhaps, but not for those most directly involved—the growing number of unemployed forest industry workers and a burgeoning army of environmental activists. Seen through their eyes, our problems go a lot deeper and are more intractable than the Premier suggests. Indeed, as Clayoquot protesters went to court in the summer of 1993 and unemployed sawmill workers from Williams Lake drove to a new mill in Hinton, Alberta in search of work, both might have tuned in to dire reports on their car radios. No, not this time about looming timber shortages on Canada's West Coast, but the disappearance of cod on the East. Perhaps this once most-teeming of all fisheries would close down completely, never to reopen. At a stroke, 25,000 people out of work, whole villages and regional communities gutted.

Everywhere the environment is in trouble; everywhere employment is stalled. We are circling the drain, yet through it all, we hear the same old remedies that led to Bonthuis's lost job and Simpson's incarceration: we must stimulate more economic growth, we must get the volume out. Bigger-and-more is the only direction we know, as if the forests and fish could take it on the chin forever.

It may sound cliché, but we are today at a crossroads. To the protester at the Kennedy Bridge, the sign points to a change in the roadway that leads over a very different landscape. To those on the road to Hinton, conventional economic thinking keeps pointing up a long, steep hill to a new place where, for the time being, we can get the wood out.

In BC, the first European settlers found a land with unlimited views of ancient forests and bountiful waters, a wealth that was treated as free for the taking. Now, a few generations later, the end of that bounty is in sight and, in many watersheds, it's already here. Yet our treatment of the environment and its resources hasn't changed accordingly. Looking back in history, we recognize that every age has, under changing circumstances, been faced with the unexpected, unwelcome challenge of radically adjusting the way it does things. In school we all learn about the Scientific and Industrial Revolutions and, standing on the after-side of this history, we understand why these revolutions occurred. Change is inevitable.

Today, the dominant fact of global life is that we are catastrophically overshooting our resource base. We take what nature provides, often at a dizzying pace, seemingly oblivious to the vastly different environment that awaits us. In Newfoundland and the other Atlantic provinces, this translates into a devastated fishing industry. In BC it translates into a "falldown" from the logging of today's old-growth forests to tomorrow's logging of much less valuable

World scientists' warning to humanity

Our massive tampering with the world's interdependent web of life—coupled with the environmental damage inflicted by deforestation, species loss, and climate change—could trigger widespread adverse effects, including unpredictable collapse of critical biological systems whose interactions and dynamics we only imperfectly understand....

We, the undersigned senior members of the world's scientific community, hereby warn all humanity of what lies ahead. A great change in our stewardship of the earth and the life on it is required if vast human misery is to be avoided and our global home on this planet is not to be irretrievably mutilated.

Union of Concerned Scientists, "World Scientists' Warning to Humanity," 1993. Signed by 1600 senior scientists from 70 countries, including 102 Nobel laureates.

Thousands of loggers and their families jeer as Premier Mike Harcourt addresses a rally in Victoria. Ian Parfitt photo.

or voluble tree plantations. If our wholesale plunder of old-growth and the social dislocation that flows from it isn't what we want, then we must change the way we live. We must embark on an Ecological Revolution, a revolution equal in scale to the great revolutions of the past, only this time we stand not after the revolution, but before it.

The consensus that eludes us

To explore the meaning of this revolution and to find creative opportunities in it is the challenge of this book. Above all, we seek to elucidate a transition strategy for the forest industry in BC that can work both environmentally and economically. Ours today is a politics where everyone is enmeshed in his own little niche, anxious to protect or advance his special interest. Take the battle for Clayoquot Sound. On the one hand, it is a struggle over our understanding of the biology that supports life, and what we know we must do to sustain ourselves and our economies. On the other hand, the conflict is about the resources that currently support a powerful industry and keep the economic juices flowing. At the CORE negotiations, the IWA worker refuses even to talk about mitigating the effects of wilderness set-asides because that would be to admit the possibility of job losses in the union. Out on the blockade, the environmental activist is concerned about one thing—preserving that area now before it is too late. Meanwhile, the Council of Forest Industries of BC has its own interest: continued profitability for its member companies. And the government struggles to provide revenues from taxes and keep the deficit down, all the while looking over its shoulder to see how distant bond markets will rate its response—and juggling the various interests in a way that accomplishes its prime goal of getting re-elected. Amidst all this, the collective social interest, like the forests and the fish, is lost. We become trapped by conflict itself.

What will it take to break past this pattern of social fragmentation and polarization? A more co-operative process for discussion is needed for sure, but so too is a more co-operative solution, an alternative that brings us together in a common quest. As one community activist told us, we are adrift in a "politics of no models": a clear vision and guide to the future are essential.

Troubled by the outcries from the environmental and labour camps, both of which lay claim to bringing electoral victory to his government, Premier Harcourt unveiled his model of the future in an historic forest policy announcement in April 1994. Called the Forest Renewal Act, the new policy of the NDP government was designed to ensure that more revenues were captured when old-growth trees were logged and then channelled back into tending the province's second-growth tree plantations. The Act, and published documents released with it, explained how the NDP planned to capture an average of 60 percent more in stumpage payments over the next five years from companies logging publicly owned forests. The extra funds—about $2 billion over five years—would help generate an estimated 5,000 to 6,000 jobs in the woods where a new and more highly trained army of workers would begin tending second-growth trees through intensive spacing, pruning and thinning work. The environmental degradation of the past—the ongoing damage to forest soils and

Misplaced loyalties

The average large business is 16,500 times larger than the average small business. And since much of the population is now employed by these large corporations, they naturally see their interest as being linked to the success and growth of their employers. Such fealty resembles the allegiance that sustained feudal baronies; the vassal serfs believed that the lord who exploited them was better than the uncertainty of no lord at all. But in the competitive world of modern commerce, loyalty to the system prevents an objective examination of how market capitalism can also work against those who serve it....

Succeeding in business today is like winning a battle and then discovering that the war was unjust. Of course, the discovery that a loyalty which has served so well can betray so badly is a troubling concept for any culture.

Paul Hawken, *The Ecology of Commerce* (New York: HarperCollins, 1993).

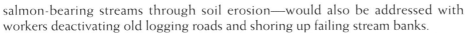
salmon-bearing streams through soil erosion—would also be addressed with workers deactivating old logging roads and shoring up failing stream banks.

Flanked by a labour leader, the head of one of the province's biggest forest companies, the mayor of a community heavily dependent on the forest industry and an environmental representative, a proud Premier Harcourt said that after months of negotiation his government had helped forge an "unprecedented partnership" that would ensure continued forest health for generations to come. "For far too long economic growth and environmental protection have been in conflict," the Premier said, adding it was time "to put back some of what we have taken away…to help make forests more productive in the future."

Unlike previous governments which made the mistake of establishing so-called "permanent" silvicultural funds without the legislated framework to back them up, the NDP enshrined their act in law. An important step had been taken to helping restore health to BC's neglected second-growth plantations. But as far as community health and the environment were concerned, many outstanding issues remained unresolved. Tenure arrangements which granted monopoly control to the biggest, most powerful forest companies in the province would remain in place along with an arbitrary, government-run timber-pricing policy that favoured the same companies in question. A more fundamental shift in provincial forest policy would have to wait for another day.

To talk about fundamental change is discomfiting, and we must guard against our own reactions. The temptation will be great for the forest industry expert to disagree with whatever is proposed, and look instead for a comforting statistical or factual error to take refuge in. Many industry critics will quickly want to call it radical and naive, perhaps ideological, and then be done with it. When we witness that reaction, we must ask ourselves: How much of it is the institutional inertia that resists and fights change? Strong though that inertia may be, we have found in our investigations something even more powerful—an emerging social consensus, however well hidden it is beneath anger and frustration. It offers us many ways to get there, and ironically, it is articulated by the very people who seem on the surface to be diametrically opposed to one another, the environmentalist and the mill worker.

Says Mark Brett: "I don't think they [MacMillan Bloedel] should have the monopoly like they do. If they're going to lay off guys, they should lose more and more of their tree farm licence. Cause they're our trees. They belong to the people….I'd say give it to the people so they can make a product, not a raw product like they do now, but a product that they can ship out. Make products like door frames, houses—whole houses, not just pieces of houses. We have done it before, but only on a small scale." Says Sile Simpson: "I think we should have a local industry, a value-added industry here, where the wood that comes out of here stays here. It stays here or the finished product is removed, traded."

The challenges that confront us

Simpson's and Brett's attitude is widely shared. In the public's disillusionment with big institutions, an underlying consensus does exist, a

---

Vanishing heritage

It has been estimated that the cumulative loss of forests in human history has been to the tune of 2 billion hectares, most of which occurred in the temperate zone. This is equivalent to the present total tropical forest area on the globe.

Hon. Shri K. R. Narayanan, Vice President of India, inaugural address delivered at First Ministerial Conference on Forestry Forum for Developing Countries (New Delhi, India, September 1–3, 1993).

Beyond polarization

Throughout the Northwest, a less-told story is emerging….A growing number of rural community residents and environmentalists are working together to try to reconcile the desires for economic vitality and environmental quality. They believe that many, if not all, of their respective goals can be achieved through cooperation; that the constant pitting of the environment against the economy will ultimately lead to the decline of both.

The most promising of these efforts do not seek a mythical "balance" between economy and environment that leaves habitats half protected, rural economies weakened, and personal principles bargained away. Instead they look to create synergies; ways that economic activity can promote a healthy environment, and that healthy ecosystems can enrich their inhabitants, economically and otherwise.

Kirk Johnston, *Beyond Polarization: Emerging Strategies for Reconciling Community and the Environment* (Seattle WA: University of Washington, Northwest Policy Center, 1993).

Left: Towering Douglas fir on Vancouver Island. Adrian Dorst photo. Right: Stacks of dimensional lumber. Gary Fiegehen photo.

consensus shared by the authors of this book. At the heart of this consensus is the need to change the direction of our forest economy from the high-volume consumption of raw resources and the rapid output of commodity lumber, pulp and paper to a value-based economy, where many fewer trees are logged but much more employment is generated making finished products. This more-from-less strategy differs fundamentally from the NDP's Forest Renewal Plan, a plan that suggests we can get more from the same amount of wood, or more from more.

In the coming three chapters we will see how today's economy depends on two broad subsidies—the erosion of our forested environment and the decline of our resource-based communities. We call this the volume economy. As it runs its course the old-growth forest resource on which it thrives will continue to be surrendered to other jurisdictions which create jobs and capture the true wealth of our forest products. If allowed to continue, this economic surrender will reach its logical conclusion with the disappearance of all accessible old-growth forests outside protected parks and wilderness areas. Under the present system of large corporate forest tenures what will be left in British Columbia is millions of hectares of second-growth forests that will be cut over every sixty to eighty years for conversion into market pulp fibre and low-quality lumber products—hardly a recipe for healthy, diverse forests or a healthy, labour-intensive industry.

In the latter half of the book we will show how this bleak future can be

The will to community

One crime I wish to name at Clayoquot Sound is the destruction of community. You who have stood before the courts, and we who have been involved in political endeavours know how passionately we can believe that what we stand for is right, and what the other side stands for is wrong and demonic. I see at Clayoquot Sound a challenge to refuse to engage in the demonizing of others, a challenge to the will to community, to do the miracle that the trees do, to breathe mercy and oxygen into the choking complexities and to transform enemies into friends. It's a challenge to forge human links in a human chain between loggers responsible to their families, environmentalists responsible to earth's ecosystems, government leaders responsible to economic realities, corporate giants responsible to shareholders, courts responsible to the upholding of laws.

Joy Kogawa, presentation at Writers for Clayoquot Sound festival (Vancouver, 1993).

avoided if only we start to change our focus now, toward what we call the value economy. The value-driven future we advocate is not abstract or unattainable. Indeed, we see examples of it every-where today, albeit on a small scale. Many people are working in the woods, taking out fewer trees than in conventional clear-cutting methods. And they're employing a lot more people per volume of wood than the highly mechanized logging methods so extensively employed today. Similarly, in small pockets across BC we see people milling that wood in ways that generate four times more employment than in conventional commodity lumber mills. If they can do it, so can others.

But Forestopia goes beyond the much-vaunted promise of alternative logging and value-added manufacturing. It extends to the promise of dramatically increased returns for the old-growth and second-growth trees logged on public lands, an attractive prospect for a provincial government mired in debt and rocked by international trade challenges to the low timber-cutting fees it exacts from forest companies. It extends to a completed parks and wilderness system and the growing tourism jobs that generates. And finally, it extends to a new approach to economic development where a range of sources of capital investment are harnessed to unleash the untapped potential of local economies. As it stands, the towns that could disappear are losing more than just the natural resources that have sustained them over the past decades. Equally unsettling, they're losing the capital investment that would allow them to diversify. The flow of natural resources out of communities is being mirrored by an exodus of investment capital, all of which spells disaster for resource-dependent towns. Properly harnessed, capital can be reinvested locally to help keep goods and services circulating within smaller communities.

Most British Columbians agree that we cannot go on as we are, that we need a different concept of our future, and a new model of development to get there. To achieve it, we must not just forecast our future from unquestioned trends of the present, but envision the possibility of a very different future, a Forestopia that will resolve present differences. From that ideal future we can then step back to the present where we can begin to make the kinds of changes now that will lead us to that better world. This book is addressed to all those people who share our hopes for breaking past our stalemate into a workable future. Today, across British Columbia, examples exist of better ways of doing things. But they are the exception to the rule. It's time to bring those successful experiments at the margin home.

CHAPTER TWO

MARCH OF THE FELLER BUNCHER

F EW THINGS DISTURB GRAHAM MORGAN MORE THAN
watching logging trucks whiz by his home on Gitwangak reserve bound
for sawmills in New Hazelton, Smithers or Terrace. The traffic is a
constant reminder of the fate of the local mill that once employed 58
people from the reserve, but was recently closed by Westar Timber Ltd.

Life on Gitwangak reserve isn't easy. But in the not too distant past it was
a lot better than today. In 1970 a sawmill opened, bringing employment to 58
men on the reserve. Another 40 people, Native and non-Native, also found
jobs at the mill, driving into work from Moricetown,
Hazelton and Smithers. Many men broke their
debilitating dependency on alcohol. Family and
community life improved and, for a while, things
were fine. But in 1989 Westar closed the mill. Band
members have fought the closure ever since, but to
no avail. Despite promises by Westar to keep it open
in return for government-granted logging rights, the
company refused to operate the mill for all but a few
months over the intervening years. The Ministry of
Forests eventually cancelled Westar's Tree Farm
Licence (TFL). But that's little comfort to the band,
which has no way of knowing if it will ever take
back control of the trees surrounding Gitwangak.

Morgan and others on Gitwangak reserve feel
betrayed, done in by an industry and government
that excluded them from the table. When Westar
received Ministry of Forests approval to build
Carnaby, a giant sawmill near New Hazelton, band members feared the worst.
How, they wondered, could Carnaby co-exist with smaller mills in the region
which depended on the local forests for their logs? Gitwangak band members
never got the answer to that question from Ministry of Forests and industry
officials. Instead, they sat on the sidelines watching their worst fears become
reality. Carnaby opened. Gitwangak closed.

Graham Morgan outside the empty expanse of the Gitwangak mill. Ian Lindsay photo.

Opposite: The cold efficiency and brute strength of a feller buncher in action. Herb Hammond photo.

Working through the forest. A feller buncher near Kamloops. Al Harvey photo.

"I don't think we'd be in this situation today if we'd been involved in the harvesting of timber and planning," Morgan says. "I think every community should have that kind of involvement because big companies have too much control themselves. They control all the data on the TFLs. They do all the planning. If the workers themselves in the community are involved, then communities that have lost jobs like we did wouldn't be in this kind of predicament. Because the timber belongs to the people, not the companies."

Several hundred kilometres to the southeast of Gitwangak on the high, dry Chilcotin plateau, where seasonal extremes have created a majestic and vital landscape, Dave Neads watches the same process unfolding outside his front door. Since the mid-1980s, loggers have reached ever further into one of the province's most spectacular landscapes to gather fuel for the burgeoning demands of several mills in Williams Lake. One dark morning a few years ago, Neads stepped out onto his porch and saw an apparition —in fact, a whole bunch of apparitions. "They looked like spaceships, tiny lights above the forest, lots of them on the hillside." Not spaceships, these were the powerful night lights of feller bunchers that had arrived on his remote doorstep, 300 km from Williams Lake.

Feller bunchers are powerful machines. Robotically grabbing whole trees, they squeeze, strip, slice and throw them down in a quick, single operation. Swarms of these machines now roar across the Chilcotin's lodgepole pine forests, cutting down record numbers of trees under special permits granted by the Ministry of Forests. Their awesome strength and speed is something few city-dwellers can comprehend. But there's no denying their cold mechanical efficiency. They are the very embodiment of the economic productivity that we so relentlessly

Were the Luddites right?

There has been a silly myth that we can keep giving jobs to machines and new, meaningful jobs will replace the old ones. It is now clear that this is not true. The "everything is temporary—take nothing for granted" new economy will continue to produce an inner conviction of insecurity and uselessness. This is obviously dangerous and expensive in human and financial terms. There is a steady rise in crime, substance abuse, family violence, violence among young people, teenage suicide, homelessness, soup kitchens and food banks. The reason for this dismal picture is directly connected to a growing lack of meaningful work. Next to the family, it is work and the relationship established by work that are the true foundations of society. If the foundations are unsound, how could society be sound? Unless we change our philosophy, this trend seems tragically unstoppable. First should come the values, *then* should come the technology.

The Luddites were a group in England who strongly protested the displacement of hand work by industrial textile machines. They correctly predicted the end of a way of life and destruction of the vitality of their towns and villages. Although the Luddites' tactics and timing were off, they were right. Their displacement and destruction has now reached a global scale....

Robert Bateman, open letter to CBC radio (1993).

pursue—productivity based on high inputs of capital, low inputs of labour and lots of resource going through. This is exactly the same sort of big-scale efficiency that shut the Gitwangak sawmill down.

It's high-volume, low-labour logging like this that has provided much of the wood for five giant sawmills in Williams Lake. But one of the five mill owners, Weldwood of Canada Ltd., recently decided to close down its sawmill anyway, doing away with 100 high-paying jobs. Many of the men and women to lose their jobs, which pay an average of $35,000 a year before benefits, are moving to Hinton, Alberta where Weldwood operates a new mill near a coniferous forest that has yet to be logged. "The company made it available for me to transfer up there and keep my holiday pay," says Gilbert King, a Weldwood employee. "And they're going to give me severance pay to help move. That's pretty hard to turn down when you're looking at what's here."

King, an IWA-Canada member, moved to Williams Lake in 1971 and began work at the Weldwood mill in 1976. The decision to close the mill, he says, is quite simple: "the wood supply is getting smaller." Small enough that people like Neads believe another sawmill in town may soon follow Weldwood's lead. But Neads doesn't expect that to translate into less logging. Rather, he says, Weldwood will retain logging rights in the area, cut the trees down and send them elsewhere for processing. "It's time to start thinking about that," Neads says. "One hundred fewer people employed. Who receives the benefit of that? And who's paying the cost?"

Of boom and bust

Neads and Morgan aren't alone in asking these questions. In resource-dependent towns across BC, many people are alarmed by job losses and the erosion of the province's once vast old-growth forests. Worried about timber leaving their regions to be processed elsewhere, concerned about "plans" that don't reflect their vision of a healthy environment and economy, people are starting to insist their communities be more involved in decisions that affect them. There's a growing realization that forests are finite, that communities would be better off realizing that now, and preparing for it. If they don't, present trends point to a difficult future regardless of environmental pressures. Indeed, the downturns both men witnessed are, in neither case, caused by wilderness preservation. Says Neads of Weldwood's closure: "It was a corporate decision that had nothing to do with environmental issues. There was no park created that impacted on timber supply."

Since World War Two, BC's growth has been fuelled by its forests. For a century before that, loggers cut down big trees, but the industry itself was tiny compared to today's standards. Since the war, logging levels have skyrocketed by over 600 percent. As logging escalated, companies consolidated, shutting down a multitude of small mills and opening larger mills with bigger appetites for wood. It was a tumultuous time for small town BC, especially with the introduction of pulp mills.

Mollie Harrington, a one-time business analyst in Quesnel, says when the pulp mill went in, "the population just boomed. Before that there were hundreds and hundreds of small mills, a very diverse economy, farmers, ranchers, people living off the land. It sent a shock through the whole system with pulp mills and larger sawmills going in and the tenure being bought up. It created a single-industry town, on top of what had been a traditional rural community." Kevin McElvey, chairman of Quesnel's Community Futures program and a colleague of Harrington's, notes the dangerous legacy of this trend. In the early 1950s, McElvey says, most boys old enough to wield a chain saw or stand on the line at a local sawmill "could drop out of school at

In the wake of the feller buncher. Row upon row of felled and bunched trees west of Nimpo Lake. Randy Stoltmann photo.

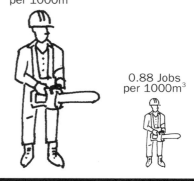

The Jobs Go Down...
Jobs created per one thousand cubic metres, 1961–91

2 Jobs per 1000m³

0.88 Jobs per 1000m³

1961   **1991**

...While The Cut Goes Up
Annual cut levels, 1961–91

74,000,000m³

32,000,000m³

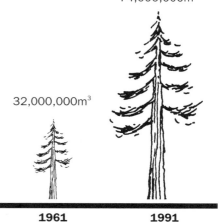

1961   **1991**

Source: Statistics Canada, Ministry of Forests Annual Reports.

any time and get a family man's job and good wages. Consequently, the people who are getting laid off today are pretty highly undereducated."

While logging climbed throughout the 1960s and '70s, industry jobs began to dip in Quesnel and other logging towns. The industry was changing, getting more productive. For cities and towns throughout BC, the effect of this modernization hit home the next decade when logging levels climbed to all-time highs and forest companies cut jobs at a rate of more than 2,000 a year.

This trend comes as no surprise to economists and forestry experts. Professor David Haley of the University of BC's School of Forestry notes that the history of forestry in BC is a history of the "constant decline of the number of jobs per unit of volume of wood. Employment is down since the early '60s, and much of that fall has been due to capital replacement of labour." Back in 1950, for example, 28 truckloads of wood created 2.3 direct jobs. By 1986 that same volume of wood couldn't even support one full-time job. "We probably have the most capital-intensive, labour-extensive lumber industry in the world," says Haley.

BC pulp mills like this one in Prince Rupert enjoyed handsome profits during the late 1980s as prices hit record highs. But new and cheaper alternate fibres, including recycled newsprint, are prompting BC companies to think about moving closer to the large "urban forests" in regions like California. Gary Fiegehen photo.

This precarious dependence marks the history of dozens of towns and cities across the province. While most people passingly familiar with BC's forest industry know that it's a major employer, generating 86,600 direct jobs (including full-time and seasonal) and a similarly large number of indirect jobs, few realize how significant a role it plays in the economic life of dozens of cities and towns. More than one-third of 55 municipalities reviewed by the Forest Resources Commission, an independent commission operating from 1989 to 1992, received over 30 percent of their total income from forestry. And it's many of those same communities that now pay the cost of years of mechanization in the industry.

Between 1981 and 1992, the total number of jobs in BC increased from 1.27 million to 1.51 million. In the forest industry, however, the trend was the reverse. From an employment base of 111,000 in 1981, the industry shed 24,400 jobs in 11 years. By the end of 1992 only 86,600 workers were left working in the forests, sawmills and pulp mills of BC. High-paying union woodworking jobs were the hardest hit, with many IWA–Canada locals reporting a halving of union jobs during the period. In Port Alberni, IWA–Canada Local 1–85 says its membership declined from 6,300 to 3,200. Large sawmills that once employed 1,200 workers now employ 350. In the major wood manufacturing centre of Vancouver, IWA jobs declined from 5,000 to 2,500.

The old-styled productivity trap

The effect of the productivity formula on jobs reveals itself in the scenes Morgan and Neads describe: mega-mills and monster machinery in pursuit of the last expanses of forest. With productivity and hence profitability based on the simple formula of cutting and processing more and more wood with ever fewer people, the situation for timber-dependent communities is becoming desperate. The statistics are staggering, the pace frightening. Over one-half of all the wood logged in the province has been cut since the mid-1970s, less than twenty years. In the Cariboo, half of the timber cut has been cut in the last eight years. The forest companies must keep up with their competitors, no matter who or where they are. In the productivity race, there is no finish line.

Troubling as these trends are, industry and government insist this is the

Last to the finish line

Chemainus, British Columbia on southern Vancouver Island has become known as "the little town that did." In 1983, the old MacMillan Bloedel sawmill that had been the mainstay of the area's economy since 1875 shut down permanently. In 1959, it had employed 950 hourly people; at the time of the shutdown there was a total of 600 personnel. The company started up the new mill in January 1985 with two shifts; by September it was up to three, with 124 hourly and 19 salaried personnel. There are now 148 hourly and 23 salaried people working at the mill. These people are working towards a stated common goal—"to be the last sawmill operating on the coast"!

Western Wood Products Forum, *Human Resources in the British Columbia Wood Products Industry* (1992).

way things must go. It is, for example, the blunt message of a telling 1992 federal report prepared for Michael Wilson by the "Forest Sector Advisory Council." A product of the scions of big labour and big industry (it was signed by Jack Munro, former IWA–Canada president, and George Petty, Chief Executive Officer of Repap International Inc.), its principal recommendations speak baldly of facilities that must close and companies that must "merge, consolidate and enter into partnership agreements in order to rationalize and compete in a global industry. Governments should not intervene, but should work with us." What the document doesn't say is that this consolidation is the inevitable result of companies building huge mills with appetites for wood far in excess of what the country's forests can provide, even if every stick of old-growth outside of parks is logged. Merely shedding excess milling capacity is expected to entail the loss of some 25,000 direct jobs.

Forestry brass talk in glowing terms of this modernization and the move to competitiveness, but the result has been the steady loss of accessible old-growth timber and the virtual collapse of whole segments of the industry such as the coastal plywood sector. Thousands of people, many of them in the Lower Mainland, used to work in plywood mills along the Fraser River. At its height in 1978, 7,750 workers were employed full-time in the coastal plywood industry. Today that number is just over 500. Making matters worse, plywood production is very labour-intensive, generating up to three times as many jobs as modern sawmills using the same amount of wood. Interior plywood mill workers haven't been hit as hard. But they too are watching jobs disappear as highly mechanized equipment gobbles up more wood with fewer workers. Jymm Kennedy, an environmental officer with Local 25 of the Pulp, Paper and Woodworkers Union, comments: "Three years ago North Central Plywood [in Prince George] put in a new lathe. On one eight-hour shift it can produce as much as two machines in three shifts. It's the fastest-running lathe in the world. Six jobs are gone and they're producing more."

For timber-dependent communities like Prince George, Williams Lake or Port Alberni, the toll on jobs was exacted long before Clayoquot Sound became a high-profile issue. The Alberni Valley had one of the highest per capita incomes in Canada until the late '70s, but was floored by the recession of the 1980s, and never recovered. The region lost approximately 2,000 jobs in a year and a half. So serious was the situation that a Special Job Protection Commissioner for Port Alberni was appointed. Robert Wood's report painted a bleak and accurate picture of what lay ahead for besieged loggers and mill workers in Port Alberni, forecasting the loss of some 1,340 full-time jobs. Of those jobs losses, 1,100 occurred as a result of MacMillan Bloedel Ltd. closing or downsizing various operations. "The double tragedy," Wood said, "is that most of these jobs will not be recovered within the primary forest sector."

After a frenzied if misdirected expansion in the 1980s, the pulp and paper sector is also in dire straits in the '90s, some of its output rendered irrelevant by paper recycling in major newsprint-consuming regions like California and by faster-growing trees in southern climes. Again it is communities like Port Alberni that pay the price. In late 1993, MacMillan Bloedel ended kraft pulp production at Port Alberni, causing a further loss of 200 jobs. At MB's Port Alberni and Powell River pulp and paper operations, the Communications, Energy and Paperworkers Union of Canada will have lost between 800 and 1,000 members from the beginning of 1993 to the end of 1994. The company has recently announced it will build western North America's first lightweight coated paper machine in Port Alberni at an estimated cost of $200 million. However, the new machine will produce only 30 jobs (that's over $6 million per job), something Vicky Husband of the

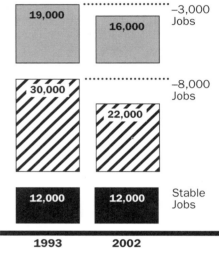

Not A Growth Industry

Employment projections by major forest companies.

19,000   16,000   –3,000 Jobs

30,000   22,000   –8,000 Jobs

12,000   12,000   Stable Jobs

1993   2002

☐ Logging And Silviculture

▨ Manufacturing

■ Remanufacturing / Value Added

Source: Western Wood Products Forum, Human Resources in the Solid Wood Products Sector (1993).

Sierra Club calls characteristic of the "jobless growth" experienced in many forest industry towns in BC today.

As a result of the massive job losses and the paltry job gains made through new capital investments, a siege mentality has set in in the ranks of the woodworking and pulp and paper unions. In many towns there's only one big employer, and that employer controls most of the means of production and most of the region's forests. Occasionally the union calls for the government to take a company's logging rights away if it isn't prepared to maintain jobs. But more often than not it ends up siding with the company, particularly when it comes to land withdrawals for new parks or wilderness areas such as Clayoquot. As Dave Steinhauer, second vice-president of IWA–Canada 1–85 puts it: "We figure about 600 jobs will be lost with the Clayoquot decision. If there's going to be further job loss, I figure it's going to be due to further environmental pressures put on the government. I know the community of Ucluelet is getting really fed up with what's going on up there. Most of the people that work up there work in the forest industry. In Ucluelet if you're laid off as a logger where do you go?"

Ongoing, widespread job loss

The estimate of 11,000 people displaced from the British Columbia [wood product] industry as a whole [by the year 2,002] is conservative as it relates to an annual allowable cut level of 60–65 million m^3. Since employment dependence on the industry is particularly high in rural communities, that displacement will be widely dispersed throughout the small towns and rural municipalities of British Columbia...additional jobs lost will be in the 20,000 to 25,000 range. Again, many of these will be in rural British Columbia and they will form part of the pattern of ongoing widespread employment deterioration....In total the conservative job loss figure could be between 30,000 and 40,000 people in British Columbia.

This job loss is going to reshape the social infrastructure of rural British Columbia. There will be a loss of tax revenues at federal, provincial and municipal levels. There will be increased costs to unemployment and welfare programs. There will be default on mortgages, non-payment of rent and a high degree of insecurity and uncertainty in many small towns throughout the province.

Western Wood Products Forum, *Human Resources in the British Columbia Wood Products Industry* (1992).

WEDNESDAY 19th June 1991

Alberni Valley Times

WEATHER Sunny

Port Alberni BC

35 Cents plus GST

Vol. 42 – No. 118

Union says "Enough is enough."

Local 1-85 wants MB out of TFL 44

By ROB DIOTTE
Alberni Valley Times Editor

Local 1-85 of the International Woodworkers of America-Canada has called for MacMillan Bloedel to be removed as title holder of Tree Farm Licence 44.

In a full-page advertisement carried on page 14 in today's Times, 1-85 says, "The job losses are intolerable.

"Enough is enough," the union says.

1-85 says there were 1,800 direct and indirect forestry jobs lost in the downturn of 1982-83. The union expects to see 700 to 1,000 jobs lost in the current downsizing by MacMillan Bloedel in the Alberni Region.

"How many job losses do we experience before we challenge MacMillan Bloedel's right to tenure?" the union asks in the advertisement.

Company and local union negotiators have been going over a list of logging practices in the TFL which the company says exist here and in none of their other operations in other areas. The result has been an increase in the logging costs between $10 and $12 a cubic metre, according to company records.

MB's Alberni Region management announced in May the company would walk away from the TFL, turning back the public portion, if it could not get these practices changed and the logging costs in line with other areas. One-third of the TFL is privately-owned land held by the company.

Tensions between the two parties may have reached an impasse with the call for MB to be stripped of the TFL here.

More timber

Vandals on the rampage

Vandalism to Malaspina

The social subsidy

If Steinhauer and the worker-inspired Share groups are circling the wagons, so too are a host of other people who want to protect ways of life that aren't compatible with today's high-extraction, high-output logging and sawmilling. Gerry Bracewell is a seventy-one-year old wilderness lodge operator and guide outfitter at Tatlayoko Lake in the Chilcotin. She's also an avid supporter of selective logging and local control of resources. The way

**Hauling logs for export, Stewart, BC.
Myron Kozak photo.**

Bracewell sees it, people in her sparsely populated part of the province have a better understanding of the resources necessary to sustain the local mixed economy than the big forest company and Ministry of Forests officials in distant Williams Lake or Victoria.

In 1985 when the feller bunchers arrived and logging started to escalate in the western reaches of the Williams Lake Timber Supply Area, Bracewell and others saw trouble: "The guide outfitters pleaded with the government. It didn't make a bit of difference. You know, we're at the bottom of the scale. With the government, logging is everything. So the roads were cut into the nucleus of the moose habitat where they raised their little ones. And pretty soon all the cows were shot. The government was very slow to respond and close the roads to hunters.

"They're closing a few of them now. But it's too late. Guess what they did this year! They put the guide outfitters, the stewards of the wilderness in the Cariboo–Chilcotin, on moose quota. We have one moose a year."

Bracewell and Steinhauer may see the world from different eyes. But both care deeply about their communities, and neither likes what he sees happening around him. For both, one of the most disturbing aspects of the industry's evolution has been the growing exodus of local resources to centres far away from where they live. Not only are mills closing in places like Port Alberni, but many of the trees logged in the region—including Clayoquot—are processed in distant centres like Vancouver. This simply widens the gulf

On The Skids

*Declining Population Of Timber Towns
From 1981 To 1991*

Fort St. James	−9.89%
Gold River	−2.65%
Houston	−7.47%
Mackenzie	−1.60%
Midway	−3.48%
Pemberton	* 78.01%
Port Alice	−18.78%
Port Clements	** 27.11%
Port McNeil	6.75%
Powell River	−3.22%
Sayward	−15.77%
Slocan	−25.07%
Tahsis	−39.45%
Zeballos	−33.13%

Source: Ray Travers, "An Analysis of the Economic Transition Issues Driving the Development of a New Forest Policy for British Columbia" (Sierra Club of Western Canada, 1993).

* This increase in population growth has coincided with the rapid growth of nearby Whistler, a major tourist destination.

** In 1982, MacMillam Bloedel closed the nearby Justatla logging camp and the people were moved into town.

Problems with bigness

The proponents of corporate concentration, bureaucratic centralism, executive-dominated unions and single crop forests all, of course, deny their obsession with centralism. They argue that these methods of organization and management are efficient, economic and rational, that bigness is not pursued for its own sake, that monoculture is not an end in itself. But somehow three or four decades of so-called progress have failed to convince the skeptical. Increasing evidence suggests that neither the forms of organization nor the established theories and practices of forest management are efficient, economic or ecologically sound.

Ken Drushka, *Stumped: The Forest Industry in Transition* (Vancouver: Douglas & McIntyre, 1985).

Wooden noodles outside a spaghetti mill near Clinton. Al Harvey photo.

between BC's two economies: an urban economy of private wealth supported by cheap resources extracted from remote areas, and a rural economy that is dying and is increasingly a drag on the whole system.

The social costs associated with this economic strategy are legion. As some workers lose their jobs, those who still have them angrily reject changes proposed from the outside, clinging to the familiar if false promises of their Vancouver-based employers. Young people leaving high school see no future in town and move out, leaving a town that is increasingly without children. Unemployed families lose their houses, default on loans and stop buying from local businesses. Alcohol and drug abuse rise, domestic violence and crime become endemic and a sense of despair takes over. Mollie Harrington has seen it all in Quesnel. "There's a really significant alcohol rate and a really high level of mental illness. There's a high level of family violence," she says. Dr. Tom Strong, a psychologist at a northern regional mental health centre in Smithers, adds: "Hearing that the area sawmills have only a few years of timber left, and that this type of prognosis is common throughout the north, leaves me feeling as though I am at the base of an avalanche chute just waiting for the big one."

For Graham Morgan and others in communities stringing between Smithers and Gitwangak, the avalanche has already descended, sweeping away jobs, undermining the local resource base, sapping small communities of their vitality, taking away the hope that sustains family life. Faced with the loss of jobs and the extension of logging roads ever farther into lands they claim, some Gitksan have stood up against forest companies in an effort to regain control of their land. "The series of blockades that I've been working on, and the court actions against the Crown, they are all interrelated to bring attention to this scenario that's taking place right now," says Don Ryan, spokesman for the Gitksan and Wet'suwet'en hereditary chiefs. "Your whole economic theory has been that here's an infinite set of resources and what you try to do is build industries around that infinite resource. When that infrastructure collapses, what do you do?"

In most cases, move on, taking what little wood is left to another town where another mill, already short of timber, takes whatever it can get from wherever it can get it. Today, the unemployment rate at Gitwangak is 65 percent and alcohol and drug abuse are rampant. "I've seen, especially in the very, very young children—teenagers under fifteen—starting to drink openly," Morgan says. "And drugs are very hard to control now. It's a lot more open now than when we were all employed. And that's because the parents are drinking now. Some men have to leave their families at home. And when the father's gone, the teenagers are hard to control, particularly if the mother's working part-time."

The way Morgan sees it, the same sort of trouble looms in communities all along the northwest from Vanderhoof to Prince Rupert as sawmills compete for a diminishing supply of trees. The remaining logs "will probably go to the higher-populated areas rather than Hazelton or Gitwangak or even Smithers. I believe, myself, that the mill that took our logs away will eventually be shut down." And with that another community will suffer. For Morgan and others the only way out of this downward spiral is for local communities to stop providing a social subsidy to a distant urban economy. Only then can they begin to play a greater role in what happens to the forests surrounding them. Only then might the undermining of community economies and the erosion of the surrounding environment be reversed.

But time is running out.

Racing through the resource

In 1950 we were [harvesting an average] 22 million cubic metres. Over the past decade we've been averaging about 80 million plus cubic metres. When I scale log trucks, a highway truck will have about 30 cubic metres on it. A big off-highway truck will have anywhere from 60 to 90 cubic metres on it, depending on how crazy the loader is. To put 80 million cubic metres in terms you can actually think of, if you took a stack of lumber a metre high and a metre wide, you could circle the equator twice—that's 80 million cubic metres. We're cutting that every year, and we've done that over the past decade.

Jim Pine, quoted in *Report of Proceedings of the Select Standing Committee on Forests, Energy, Mines and Petroleum Resources* (Issue 7, Victoria. January 11, 1993).

CHAPTER THREE

DEATH OF A FOREST

E ARLY IN THE MORNING AT THE OLD TRADING POST IN NEW
Denver, two young women stand over a portable computer working the
glitches out of a troublesome program, while in another room someone
moves images of old-growth forests, second-growth plantations and pulp
mills about on a visual display terminal. From her seat at a long table covered
with government reports, press clippings and files, Colleen McCrory, an
internationally renowned environmental activist, reaches for a ringing telephone.

Minutes later she hangs up and laughs. It appears her old nemesis, former
IWA–Canada president Jack Munro, is heading to Brazil on a "fact-finding
mission" with one-time Greenpeace activist Patrick Moore. Both men are
directors of the forest company-financed Forest Alliance of BC, and both are
headed to Amazonia because of McCrory who, months earlier, published an
unflattering tabloid on Canadian forest practices called "Brazil of the North."
Predictably, Moore and Munro will return to BC to denounce the comparison,
and McCrory's already preparing her next move. "You know, I've been thinking
maybe I should issue an apology to Brazil. Things aren't as bad there as they are
here," she says.

Outside McCrory's office, it's a crisp autumn afternoon. The winds have
blown away the morning cloud and rain to offer a spectacular view of Slocan
Lake and the snow-capped mountains gracing its far shore. The slopes, whose
lower reaches are covered in unlogged forest, are part of Valhalla Park, a 49,600-
hectare wilderness area McCrory was instrumental in protecting. Like other
environmental activists, she's fighting a rearguard action to save more of the
province's unique wilderness areas at a time when BC's old-growth forests are
clearcut at a rate of about 200,000 hectares a year.

Cut, and cut, and cut

The environmental battles are most pronounced on BC's coast where
logging has taken place the longest, and where options to protect large intact
watersheds of old-growth are diminishing far more rapidly than in the vast
Amazonian rain forest. Most residents of BC take their temperate rain forests for
granted but, in fact, it is a very rare treasure, stretching along a narrow band of
the mainland coast, Vancouver Island and the Queen Charlottes. The Amazon,
by comparison, still has a rain forest the size of the continental US. As Wade
Davis, a noted ethnobotanist, says of our rapidly diminishing coastal old-growth:

Colleen "Brazil of the North" McCrory.

*Opposite: Progressive clearcut at Escalante
on the west coast of Vancouver Island. Years
after logging, the landscape still bears the
scars of industrial forestry. And further scars
are being added, with new logging in 1993.
Garth Lenz photo.*

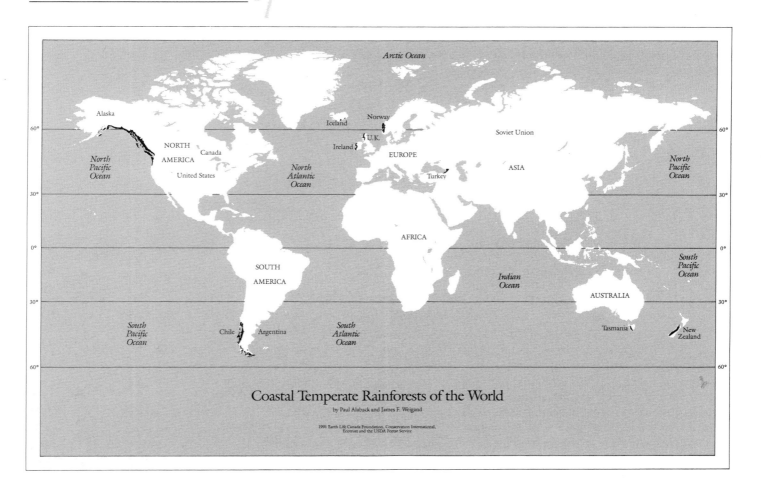

Coastal Temperate Rainforests of the World

by Paul Alaback and James F. Weigand

1991 Earth Life Canada Foundation, Conservation International,
Ecotrust and the USDA Forest Service

How rare it is

Coastal temperate rain forests constitute a relatively rare forest type, originally covering 30 to 40 million hectares, less than 1/5 of 1 percent of the earth's land surface....Of those that remain, the largest undeveloped tracts are found in South America and North America. In North America, no intact, unlogged watersheds of any size remain in the continental United States. The largest areas of undeveloped coastal temperate rain forests in the more productive zone of this biome exist in British Columbia.

Ecotrust and Conservation International, "Coastal Temperate Rain Forests: Ecological Characteristics, Status and Distribution Worldwide" (Occasional Paper Series No. 1, Abstract, 1992).

"It is a world that is far older, far richer in its capacity to produce the raw material of life, and far more endangered than almost any region of the Amazon."

International condemnation of clearcut logging in temperate rain forests has reached its zenith in places like Clayoquot Sound. Yet British Columbia's less majestic interior forests are also disappearing at an astonishing rate. In fact, about 70 percent of all the timber logged in the province each year comes from interior forests. And because these forests contain trees of a much smaller size than those on the coast, more land area is cleared to supply the volume of wood needed to feed local mills. In the Bowron Lakes region, one continuous clearcut sprawls over 20,000 hectares of land. Many clearcuts in BC's interior also span sensitive habitat: at the confluence of the Bowser and Bell-Irving Rivers in northwestern BC, a once-lush valley bottom spreading over more than 6,000 hectares has been stripped of all its spruce trees.

These are the mistakes of the past, we are told by our provincial government. They will never be repeated because the government is committed to bringing down the size of clearcuts. But if cutblocks abut each other, if they are separated by only tiny fringes of trees, the result is still large-scale clearcutting of valley bottoms and mountainsides. At Grano Creek, for example, in the last five years eleven cutting permits for 69 separate cutblocks, covering more than 3,000 hectares of pine forest, were issued to logging companies like Pope and Talbot Ltd. Eighty kilometres southeast of Kelowna and visible from Big White ski resort, the forests of Grano Creek are dominated by small-diameter lodgepole pine trees. From the logging roads crisscrossing this mountainside one notices small patches of trees whose needles have turned red, the result of infestations of mountain pine beetles. The ostensible reason for logging Grano Creek is to "salvage" these attacked trees before they are rendered useless for lumber production, and possibly to prevent the further attack of healthy pine forest. But the clearcutting at Grano Creek isn't following the beetle outbreak. Large stretches of healthy pine forest are being logged here as well.

To ride over this landscape is to realize just how quickly it changes after logging. The visible level of waste is astonishing. The pine forests of Grano Creek are dense and dark, filled with small-diameter pine trees that sprung from the ashes of a long-ago fire. Many trees simply aren't big enough to be run through a big sawmill and so are left on the ground after logging. Trekking through an undisturbed forest at Grano Creek, one can measure trees that naturally fell to the forest floor whose trunks are no more than 6 inches in diameter at the base. If these trees were logged, perhaps the bottom 24 feet would run through a sawmill, while the top 36 feet would be skidded to the side of the road and burned. And this is one of the larger trees, for the clearcut landscape on the other side of the road is littered with tiny stumps, many less than four inches across, the minimum size required for Pope and Talbot's mills. Elsewhere, huge walls of shattered logs lie parallel to the road like giant funeral pyres to the forest that once was, waiting for the right moment to be set ablaze. That moment will come in the fall, and the Okanagan skies will be filled with smoke for weeks on end.

Narrow leave strips provide scant protection for streams and rivers in the Nass Valley. Gary Fiegehen photo.

On mountain after mountain, in valley after valley throughout the province, this scene is repeated with official plans calling for the wholesale logging of large tracts of valley bottom forest over one or two passes. In Chetwynd, Wayne Sawchuk, a former logger turned environmentalist, protests current plans submitted by Tackama Forest Products to the Ministry of Forests. The plans call for extensive clearing of softwood valley-bottom forests along one of Canada's grand rivers of the north, the Liard. Half the trees in the lowlands will be logged in the first pass, says Sawchuk. "And they are leaving the timber on the side of the slopes for the second pass, so essentially what you have is stripping the entire valley bottom." In nearby hardwood forests much the same thing is happening, only the level of waste is even higher. Almost two-thirds of the hardwood trees coming down in the forests near Fort Nelson never make it through the local chopstick mill. Deemed aesthetically unpleasing, the rejected wood is hauled to the side of the road and set ablaze, just like at Grano Creek.

By the government's own admission, today's logging rate greatly exceeds that which is sustainable. In 1991–92, 74.9 million cubic metres of wood was extracted from BC's forests, although the official estimate of the Long Run Sustained Yield (LRSY) is only 59 million cubic metres. Worse yet, the ministry's estimate of what is sustainable is itself optimistic. Predictions of timber growth in plantations are unsubstantiated. And inventory data of standing timber, the information used to justify today's logging rates, is so out of date that the Forest Resources Commission called it a disgrace. Silvicultural activity such as thinning and pruning is deemed not economic to undertake and is vastly inadequate, while the risk of insect infestation in even-aged plantations is high. The cumulative effect of soil erosion takes whole areas out of future production. And there is the huge uncertainty of how artificial forests will respond to the wild cards of ozone depletion and global climate change. Beyond this range of variables is the decrease in the cut level that would occur if our treatment of the forests was based on non-timber values such as the protection of biological diversity, aesthetics and recreation.

At stake here is not just the dangerously unsustainable level of logging, but the type of timber that is targeted for removal. Every year, the quality of the forest remaining is deteriorating because of the pervasive practice of high-grading—logging the best old-growth first from the most easily accessible, productive low-elevation sites. Take, for example, BC's highly prized old-growth Douglas fir and western red cedar. From the turn of the century through the 1980s, these two species provided more than one-third of all the wood logged in BC. By the early '90s, Douglas fir comprised only 6.5 percent of the total tree inventory and western red cedar, 9.4 percent. Not surprisingly, intact ecosystems of Douglas fir are extremely rare in the province today. This tree species is now among those most vigorously protected by environmentalists, and the one most under-represented in existing and proposed protected areas. It is also the one most valued by the forest industry, so the conflict which ensues is only natural.

These historic practices portend a future marked by both a declining quality and a higher cost of timber, and an inevitable ratcheting down of cut levels, the so-called falldown which is already upon us. Seventy-four percent of foresters surveyed in a recent federal study believed that a problem was looming nationally, and that it was most severe in BC, where almost half said the prospects for sustainability were poor. This explains why, with every recalculation of the forest inventory, the provincial government is steadily bringing logging levels down in timber supply areas across the province.

University of BC forestry professor David Haley says a "very, very significant drop" in annual logging levels to between 55 and 60 million cubic metres may soon come. But others go even further. Tom Bradley, a forest technician with Silva Ecosystem Consultants, says that "we are talking about reducing the allowable annual cut by 50 percent [i.e. 36 million cubic metres or 1.02 million truckloads per year]. The ugly part is that in many specific locations in BC we have gone past the threshold of sensible and responsible management in the past ten or fifteen years....At a landscape level, in many places, we have already cut everything that should be cut and we've done it in less than half a rotation. And we aren't slowing down."

But beyond the economic discussion—how much wood is left for the industry to cut—are the environmental implications of this trend, equally unsettling for our immediate and long-term future. That level of cut comes from somewhere—from a natural forest that is everywhere being stripped, degraded and broken up.

The conveyor belt to oblivion

In the 1940s when sustained yield was first applied, the forests contained mainly slow-growing mature and over-mature forests. They were "piled up" at the end of the conveyor and the belt was moving very slowly. A decision was made to transform the forests....The conveyor was "started" and harvest rates set such that after approximately 80 years, there would be a balance of trees of all ages up to age 80 growing at the fastest rate possible.

Since these mature forests were significantly older than 80 years, they contained an additional inventory of volume, providing society with a one-time bonus for the first crop rotation. This is why the current rate of harvest is greater than the sustainable level. It has resulted from the abundance of over-mature forests and a policy decision to achieve the conditions necessary for sustained yield in one crop rotation. Harvest rates greater than the sustainable level do not necessarily mean that the forests are being overcut nor do they mean that future sustainability is at risk.

Letter from Lois Dellert, former assistant chief forester of BC, explaining "sustainable forestry" to Ian Gill, a reporter (CBC television, February 1991).

The conveyor belt picked up speed

Overall in BC, 50 percent of the volume logged has been since 1972....In coastal regions 50 percent of the volume logged has been since 1966....In interior regions 50 percent of the volume logged has been since 1977.

O. R. (Ray) Travers, "History of Logging and Sustained Yield in BC, 1911–90," in *Forest Planning Canada* (Vol. 8, No. 1, Jan-Feb 1992).

Fragmented future

British Columbia's forests contain Canada's richest abundance of trees, mosses, plants, birds and wildlife. Large numbers of birds and animals are only found here, others exist here in their greatest proportions. Nearly three-quarters of all mammals in the country are found in BC, many of them exclusive to the province. What's more, as scientists delve into the complexity of these forests, they are discovering heretofore unknown life forms.

In one study funded by the forest ecology research program of the Ministry of Forests, species are being collected from platforms constructed by environmental volunteers high in the canopies of the old-growth Sitka spruce trees in the Upper Carmanah valley. Andy MacKinnon, the manager of the project, has been astounded at the results. "Approximately 40 percent of the species being collected are new to science. New to science, not just new to the province, but new to science."

Much of this rich plant and animal life depends on forests, sometimes in unexpected ways. Take away too much of one thing and you threaten the existence of another. The caribou habitat in the Quesnel Highlands is a good example. Harold Armleder, a wildlife habitat ecologist with the Ministry of Forests' regional office in Williams Lake, is trying to protect that habitat while at the same time allowing for limited logging. Local sawmills have run short of wood in heavily logged valley bottoms and have come to collect their booty from higher elevation forests. And that's where the trouble begins, because this higher ground contains the major winter food source for caribou. Hanging from the branches of centuries-old spruce trees, delicate strands of black and green lichen sway in the wind. In the winter the caribou will walk on packed snow beds craning their necks to pluck the lichen down.

Armleder hopes an experiment now underway in which clearcut sizes are dramatically reduced and dispersed will help preserve enough lichen to sustain

Wildlife of BC's old-growth forests

Reptiles and Amphibians (8), Status (1 red, 2 blue)
Sharptailed Snake, Pacific Giant Salamander, Tailed Frog, Rough-skinned Newt, Clouded Salamander, Ensantina Salamander, Northwestern Salamander.

Birds (41), Status (3 red, 7 blue)
Spotted Owl, Marbled Murrelet, Flammulated Owl, Ancient Murrelet, White-headed Woodpecker, Williamson's Sapsucker, Blue Heron, Bald Eagle, Grey-cheeked Thrush, Lewis's Woodpecker, Vaux's Swift, Black-backed Woodpecker, Boreal Owl, American Kestrel, Blue Grouse, Brown Creeper, Barrow's Goldeneye, Bufflehead, Hermit Thrush, Pileated Woodpecker, Osprey, Chestnut-backed Chickadee, Clark's Nutcracker, Common Merganser, Grey Jay, Great Grey Owl, Hairy Woodpecker, Olive-sided Flycatcher, Pygmy Nuthatch, Red Crossbill, Red-breasted Nuthatch, Red-breasted Sapsucker, Spruce Grouse, Townsend's Warbler, Varied Thrush, Western Flycatcher, White-breasted Nuthatch, Wood Duck, Hooded Merganser.

Mammals (28), Status (4 red, 7 blue)
Cascade Mantled Ground Squirrel, Keen's Long-eared Myotis, Fringed Myotis, Small-footed Myotis, Caribou, Roosevelt Elk, Grizzly Bear, Mountain Beaver, Northern Long-eared Myotis, Shrew-mole, Trowsbridge's Shrew, Black-tailed Deer, Mule Deer, Moose, Mountain Goat, Marten, Big Brown Bat, Silver-haired Bat, Black Bear, Long-legged Myotis, Northern Flying Squirrel, River Otter, Western Long-eared Myotis, Wolverine, Yuma Myotis, California Myotis, Little Brown Myotis.

• *"Red-listed" species are under consideration for designation as endangered or threatened.*
• *"Blue-listed" species are sensitive or vulnerable, have shown a major population decline, or their numbers and distribution are poorly known.*

Ministry of Forests, *Towards an Old-Growth Strategy* (1992).

Critical habitat

Some wildlife species require old growth forest for part or all of their habitat requirements....In these forests, it is usually the structural components, such as standing dead trees, broken-topped and decaying live trees, large fallen logs, and abundant arboreal lichens that are important to wildlife. This high structural diversity and complexity results in high overall wildlife diversity, although the density can be less than in earlier successional stages. There are at least 16 wildlife species in British Columbia that find optimal habitat in old-growth forests....

Intensive forestry with its emphasis on clearcutting and maximization of conifer production, can benefit a few wildlife species in the short term, but is detrimental to many species in the long term.

Ministry of Forests, *Ecosystems of British Columbia* (1991).

One of the worst of many bad examples of recent logging-related damage to salmon streams on Vancouver Island. John Werring photo.

the local caribou herd. But it's only a hope. Much study remains into whether even this partial logging system will disturb lichen populations in the surrounding forest. What is certain is that in those areas logged, lichens won't reappear for 100 to 150 years, according to Trevor Goward, a noted UBC lichenologist. Further, the older a forest, the more lichen you find. "If you find a forest that's 500 years old it will contain more species of lichen—including rare or unusual species of lichen—than a 300-year-old forest," Goward says.

Like the researchers in the Upper Carmanah, Goward is also finding new species. In 1987, when he drew up a checklist of lichen species found in British Columbia, he came up with about 1,100 names. In the intervening seven years he's found 100 new species. All together Goward believes the province's forests will be found to contain 1,600 species of lichens, but "we're just a long, long way from really knowing what occurs," he says.

Logging in these forests is a very risky business: take too many trees out of old-growth forests and you lose viable populations of lichen. Take too much lichen away and you force the caribou to move farther and farther away in search of food, through a landscape of nutrient-poor second-growth trees and clearcuts.

And this is but one example. A recent audit of logging on Vancouver Island revealed horrendous damage to salmon habitat as a result of careless industrial forestry. This despite the fact that the companies involved had all helped to draft and later signed guidelines to protect fish habitat from logging activity. A survey of 21 cutblocks chosen at random showed there was on average one major or moderate impact on one stream for every cutblock inspected. Thirty-five percent of 53 stream reaches suffered "complete habitat loss." Twenty-six percent suffered partial habitat loss. Over 90 percent of the streams had increased debris loads. The number of streams judged to be stable before and after logging dropped from 85 percent to 50 percent. And, the audit concluded, "most of the problems were considered avoidable." This is environmental negligence on a tragic scale.

Abuse of the salmon is only one more example of a larger phenomenon: our living heritage of biodiversity is constantly undermined by today's high logging

Slamming the salmon

The stream impacts observed during the block surveys were almost exclusively long-term changes in channel morphology that were easily visible one to four years after logging....

Thirty-four (64.2%) of the 53 stream reaches surveyed were affected to some degree....Twelve (35.3%) had major impacts, nine (26.6%) had moderate impacts, and thirteen (38.2%) showed minor impacts....

Logging appears to have caused a substantial reduction in stream stability in the cutblocks examined, partly because of the increase in the debris loads present...and partly because of the increase in sediment volumes behind debris jams. The number of streams judged to be stable before logging, based on their condition upstream in older logged or unlogged reaches above the cutblocks, dropped from 84.9% to 49.1%. The risk of further impacts to downstream reaches also appeared to have increased in 52.6% of the streams examined....

When large trees were taken right off the banks, as was commonly observed, the stabilizing quality of their root wads was also lost, which increased the potential for bank erosion....In the absence of specific prescriptions, compliance with the Coastal Fisheries Forestry Guidelines was generally poor (29.9%).

Results of an audit of 21 cutblocks chosen at random on Vancouver Island to measure compliance with the voluntary Coastal Fisheries Forestry Guidelines. Tripp Biological Consultants, *The Application and Effectiveness of the Coastal Fisheries Forestry Guidelines in Selected Cut Blocks on Vancouver Island* (1992).

levels. About 90 percent of our logging is clearcut, and virtually all of it comes from old-growth forests. Not only has this resulted in the progressive eradication of rich streamside and valley-bottom vegetation, but it has fragmented the forest landscape. The numbers are sobering. Of the 30 primary watersheds in the Lower Mainland, all are logged. Of the 54 such watersheds on the south coast, only one remained pristine as of 1992: the Paradise. That paradise is now being lost, as logging commenced in 1993. On Vancouver Island, only 5 of the 90 watersheds over 5,000 hectares remain unlogged today. Overall, of the 354 primary watersheds in coastal BC, fully 80 percent are modified or "developed" to use the official terminology. Only 6 of them are both pristine and entirely protected. Yet, as the government's own State of the Environment Report (1993) notes, these temperate rain forests "occur in a few scattered spots around the world and are considered rare on a global scale."

Merely to list the problems with current logging practices is to understand the thousand scars and injuries that we are inflicting on the landscape. As countless Western Canada Wilderness Committee posters of charred hillsides have informed us over the years, clearcutting is of paramount concern here. Site-specific forestry is a virtually dead science in BC: clearcutting is being prescribed everywhere. Far from mimicking natural disturbances, as professional foresters repeatedly claim, clearcutting quite simply replaces the whole forest. Gone is the complexity of natural forests where a towering Douglas fir stands next to a cedar sapling, and a nearby spruce provides shade to an untrammelled brook. When they are clearcut, the way these trees hold soil and recycle nutrients is ripped up, the way the rooted forest floor holds and cycles water is torn asunder, and the way the canopy moderates the local climate is sheared away. Fragmented or gone are the habitats of the owl and the caribou, while the stream channels that support trout and salmon become silted with soil and clogged with logging debris. After all this, it is ludicrous to say that replanting some trees can possibly "reforest" what was there before.

What's happening here must be understood in its baldest terms: we are raking over the land on a grand scale. This is a landscape equivalent to the once-teeming marine environment where huge factory trawlers have vacuumed up the last of the cod on the East Coast with super-efficiency. "Oops, we made a mistake," and then move on. A rash of plant, bird and animal extinctions is a sad but real possibility in many parts of BC. About one-half of all vertebrate species in BC live in the forests, and three-quarters of the mammal species require forest cover. Several types of cavity-nesting bats and birds are old-growth dependent, and cannot survive in artificial forests. Old-growth dependent birds include the spotted owl and other species of murrelet, swift and woodpecker. Caribou, Roosevelt elk, black-tailed deer, mule deer and mountain goat need old-growth. Many forest-dwelling animals are threatened with imminent extinction or local extirpation throughout all or a significant portion of their range in BC. And the sad and troubling thing is that we could be losing species we don't yet know anything about.

Washing away the wealth

The reason…for concern is that soil disturbance surveys conducted between 1976 and 1985 indicated that the area of land included in roads, landings, bladed skid roads, heavily used skid trails and backspar trails varies between 6 percent and as high as 87 percent of the harvested area. The average disturbance province-wide has been estimated to be 20 percent of the total harvest area.

What that means…is that somewhere in the neighbourhood of about 10 percent of the total area harvested over those ten years has been so degraded that it is now permanently removed from production and this represents a serious biological and economic loss to the province. In fact, the loss is so serious that, if the trend were allowed to continue, by the end of the first rotation, more productive land will have been taken out of production by routine carelessness in harvesting and silviculture, than by allocation of land into all currently existing and proposed parks and wilderness areas in the province.

John Cuthbert, Chief Forester of BC, speech delivered at College of New Caledonia Logging Seminar. Reprinted in *BCEN Report* (December 1992).

Recent roadbuilding and logging at Cold Creek in Clayoquot Sound.
Adrian Dorst photo.

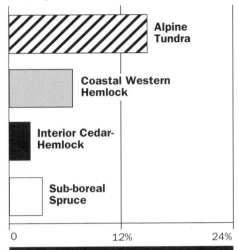

Rock and Ice

Ecosystem representation in BC parks

Alpine Tundra

Coastal Western Hemlock

Interior Cedar-Hemlock

Sub-boreal Spruce

0   12%   24%

Source: Adapted from Ministry of Environment, Lands and Parks, "Biogeoclimatic Ecosystem Classification Summary for BC Protected Areas Strategy" (updated January 29, 1994).
Note: Does not include Ts'yl-os Park. Includes Tatshenshini and Clayoquot decision. Area in parks includes fully protected and other partially protected designations.

Islands are not enough

Throughout British Columbia we confront the spectacle of a few last wild places left. In the face of this broad assault, BC's existing park system is clearly an inadequate counterbalance. Indeed, many of its parks were designed to protect scenic areas with high recreation potential but not necessarily with great biological values. Quite the contrary, the guiding principle in drawing park boundaries has often been to exclude rich old-growth areas that contain valuable timber. This so-called rock-and-ice approach goes some way to explaining why over 90 percent of Vancouver Island's alpine areas are in parks, yet less than 1 percent of the coastal Douglas fir forest is protected. Province-wide, alpine tundra and sub-alpine forests represent more than 60 percent of the parks system. Protected low-elevation forests, on the other hand, are much harder to find. It is this process which accounts for the odd shape of places like Garibaldi Provincial Park.

In an effort to protect more of BC's natural heritage, the provincial government has weighed in with a laudable plan to double parkland to cover 12 percent of the land base by the year 2,000. Unlike other regions, including the US Pacific Northwest, BC still has time to preserve significant areas of wilderness, although it would be a major feat to set aside 12 percent of the land base in parks and wilderness that included a representative sample of biodiverse valley-bottom forests. But even if the government succeeds in protecting 12 percent of the lowlands and the highlands, many ecologists point out that there are species that cannot survive in small islands of natural habitat in a sea of industrial activity. Large areas of the surrounding countryside must also be managed in a way that protects biological needs.

Perhaps the greatest irony of all is what doubling protected areas really means. We aren't, after all, creating something new on the ground. These future protected areas exist in the wild already. By designating them with lines on the map, we aren't increasing wilderness. Quite the contrary, natural areas are shrinking all the time, and the 12 percent just provides some fences around a few islands on the landscape into which the industrial machine isn't supposed to stray. And in laying out these fences, forest companies, their suppliers and employees continue to lobby to sink the posts around high-altitude rock and ice while environmental groups take to the blockades to fight for the lowland forests.

These are critically important fences to build if we are to have representative protected areas. Equally important are the Biodiversity Guidelines and the Forest Practices Code now being developed. These initiatives are a first step and will undoubtedly lead to smaller clearcuts and greater

Going, going...

There are 58 remaining undeveloped watersheds larger than 1,000 hectares on Vancouver Island....
Plans for the 58 remaining undeveloped watersheds are as follows:
- 37 are scheduled for development
- 17 are scheduled for development within 5 years

- 20 are scheduled for development within 5 to 20 years
- 21 are protected from development by their land status (e.g. park or recreation area)
- 12 of these are in Strathcona Park.

John Wilkinson, Undeveloped Watersheds on Vancouver Island Larger than 1000 Hectares (Technical report, Ministry of Forests, Recreation Branch, 1992:3, 1990).

The last generation

Protected area planning to date has failed to recognize many important special habitat features of old-growth forest and non-forest ecosystems, such as riparian ecosystems, grassland communities, wetlands, estuaries, floodplains, etc....The length, albeit the existence, of [rare, threatened and endangered species] lists illustrates that we have done a less than adequate job of protecting our wildlife habitats and species in the past.

Kaaren Lewis, Andy MacKinnon and Dennis Hamilton, "Protected Areas Planning" (Paper presented to Habitat Futures Conference: Expanding Horizons on Forest Ecosystem Management; Vernon, BC, October 21, 1992).

protection of riparian zones. But they are still in their infancy, and whether they will lead to a dramatic reduction in volume needed to protect all forest values is still very much an open question. In the volume economy that depends on the subsidy of a consumed environment, stiff resistance will greet any initiative that reduces the fibre supply to the major forest companies. As MacMillan Bloedel noted in its 1992 annual review, the company "remains committed to preserving its AAC and believes that any government regulations to reduce annual harvest levels without adequate cost–benefit analysis could be very detrimental to the economic well-being of the province." Thus, in early 1992 when the NDP government reduced MB's logging level on south Vancouver Island by 400,000 cubic metres, the company appealed the decision to a panel which re-set the cut at the level proposed in MB's management plan. Referring to the end of the term for the present NDP government, a popular industry phrase these days says it all: "Stay alive 'til '95."

Cut, run and burn. Towering piles of slash in a clearcut in the East Ootsa working forest await the torch. Will Koop photo.

Indeed, space and time are running out. And as they do, conflict rises, drawing into the fray international environmental organizations with the power to influence buyers of BC forest products. The extent of the conflict over one area like Clayoquot Sound highlights just how difficult and elusive is a meaningful 12-percent goal. But it also serves to focus our attention on the need for a transition strategy, a strategy that depends both on what we protect and on what we do on the rest of the land base.

Reducing present and future land-use conflicts will require policies that go beyond simply identifying which areas are protected and which are logged. Setting aside 12 percent of BC's land base as wilderness, while leaving the remainder open to development, isn't enough to stabilize local economies or protect the province's natural environment. Through active government intervention, BC's forest economy must be transformed in ways that ensure environmental protection across the landscape, while still providing for stable jobs. Exciting examples of such activity already exist in tiny pockets across BC. But we are perilously close to surrendering hope of their becoming anything more than the exception to the rule.

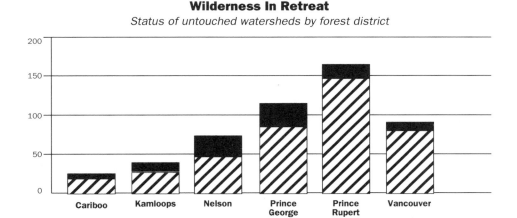

Wilderness In Retreat

Status of untouched watersheds by forest district

- ■ Untouched
- ▨ Fragmented

Source: Ministry of Forests, Recreation Branch, An Inventory of Undeveloped Watersheds in British Columbia (Technical report, 1992).

CHAPTER FOUR

ECONOMIC SURRENDER

I N STEWART, HOME TO CANADA'S NORTHERNMOST ICE-FREE
port, trucks rumble through town to dump some of the region's finest logs
into a harbour choked with booms, while somewhere in the north Pacific a
Japanese freighter steams toward BC's rugged northwest coast to fill its hold.
When the freighter arrives, a team of part-time longshoremen will grab a couple
of days of much-needed work, then settle in for another long spell of
unemployment until the next ship drops anchor. For these men, life is a waiting
game with little payoff at the end.

Eleven months into the year, in the dying days of November, David White
counts the time he's worked. "My hours to date for this year are 252.75. My
hours have dropped dramatically. So have others'." White doesn't like what he
sees happening around him. Some people make good money hauling logs out of
the forest to Stewart or distant sawmills in Terrace, but that's it. There's no mill in
Stewart. Indeed, there's not much of a port to speak of, just a gravel road jutting
into the harbour with a couple of makeshift cranes and cables to pull the logs off
the trucks and drop them in the ocean.

Stewart is a dumping ground, the end of the road, a place where people
surrender the wealth of the land to overseas buyers or distant companies in BC's
Lower Mainland. And it is symptomatic of what is wrong in a province still
endowed with some of the richest forests remaining on the planet.

The great giveaway

"It's kind of deplorable," says White as he waits for the next ship to haul
away another load to somewhere else. A proud British Columbian, White is even
sympathetic to some of what he sees, but only to a degree: "I understand how the
huge population in the Lower Mainland requires some of the north's resources to
keep its exports up. But what's happening in Stewart is that we see very little by
way of profit coming to us. And that has a direct effect on our economy. It
destabilizes our economy. I don't see much of a future for Stewart except for
mining. And I've seen several mines come and go. We end up in a recession,
while the rest of the province does just fine."

If something doesn't change, White says the forests in the nearby North
Kalum Timber Supply Area will soon be logged out and all hope of economic
diversification for his community lost. "We'll be left here with a raped
community, a raped forest, and nothing to show for it." White and others in BC's

Filling the belly of a freighter with whole logs for export. Gary Fiegehen photo.

Opposite: Skimming the cream. Log buyers walk booms of prized and increasingly rare BC Douglas fir logs in Nagoya, Japan, spring 1993. Herman Hans photo.

Every day, trucks head across the Canada–US border with partly processed wood for re-cutting in Washington and Oregon.
Steve Bosch photo.

northwest are tired of the great giveaway in which their land and resources feed the economy of a foreign nation or the Lower Mainland. But if White saw what happens to some of the logs that go to Vancouver from coastal communities like Prince Rupert or the Queen Charlotte Islands, he'd be even more alarmed. In BC's biggest city, a metropolitan centre with a huge manufacturing base, old-growth is often surrendered to foreign buyers after only the most rudimentary processing.

Harry Bains knows that well. Bains is third vice-president of the IWA –Canada's Vancouver local, a local that has lost 2,500 members in the last decade. Among those recently to join the ranks of the unemployed from Local 1–217 were 15 employees at a planer mill at Terminal Forest Products Ltd. on Mitchell Island in Richmond. The planer workers lost their jobs after Terminal invested $9 million in a small mill in nearby Everson, Washington. Terminal then started shipping six double-trailer truckloads a day of rough-cut two-by-twelve cedar lumber down to Everson where workers being paid a little more than a third the wage of their Canadian counterparts re-cut the wood into high-value cedar fencing products.

The workers who lost their jobs feel betrayed, Bains says. After all, the wood being re-cut in Washington is BC wood. People here have the know-how to do as good or better with it than workers across the Canada–US

Boards to the USA

For a number of years there has been a call for the forest industry to diversify into secondary manufacturing....Although the FTA [Free Trade Agreement] improves the access to the US market of secondary products, Canadian exports may continue to be dominated by products having a low value added component.

A more speculative issue relates to whether the industry in both countries will become dominated by a small group of large corporations, each of which has operations in both countries. Numerous mergers and take-overs are now occurring, and the possibility exists that the rate of concentration will accelerate across the international boundary because the FTA...increases the ease with which transboundary mergers and take-overs can be undertaken. Therefore, it may not be far-fetched for the industry in both countries to become dominated by the same few firms.

Should this transboundary concentration occur, it might, for example, be profitable for the industry generally to lobby for low stumpage fees in Canada and to undertake the secondary manufacturing of wood products in the US. This would permit the industry to continue investment in Canada in large, efficient mills producing standard products and would provide it with a share of the rent from forest land. It would also permit manufacturing to occur close to markets with a labour force that currently, at least, is less expensive than in Canadian labour....The flow from Canada to the United States would consist largely of products that have not gone beyond the stage of primary manufacturing, and secondary manufacturing would occur largely in the US.

Irving K. Fox, "Canada–United States Trade in Forest Products: Issues and Uncertainties," in *Emerging Issues in Forest Policy*, ed. Peter N. Nemetz (Vancouver, BC: UBC Press, 1992).

border. "I think in British Columbia we have to start to do things differently," Bains says. "I think it will take government initiative along with company willingness to accept the fact that yes, we have less fibre available. And in order to create or even sustain the jobs that we have in British Columbia we have to do more with less timber." But accomplishing that won't be easy because the strategy of many big forest companies is to move further into the volume economy. The result is that fewer and fewer jobs are created per volume of wood run through BC's mills. Just across the border the US forest industry generates three to four times as many jobs per cubic metre as does BC.

Much of the wood supporting the thriving, labour-intensive US industry comes from BC. (An estimated 40 mills in Oregon and Washington process almost exclusively raw lumber imported from the province.) Despite moves in recent years to diversify into more value-added wood products manufacturing, export of commodity lumber, pulp and paper products remains the driving engine of BC's forest industry. And this comes as no surprise. After all, the big companies that dominate the industry have a stranglehold on the land base through 20- and 25-year forest licence and tree farm licence agreements with the Crown. With licences in hand, these companies then design mills to consume wood in whatever way will turn the quickest profit. And in the volume economy, that means spitting out the most wood in the quickest time with the fewest workers.

Adding insult to injury, we have long surrendered at bargain basement prices the trees that make our lumber. Today, most logging in publicly owned forests is done by, or for, a handful of large companies who negotiated long-term logging rights with the BC government. In return for the logs, the companies pay stumpage fees to the government. Given the complex formula by which these fees are calculated, however, they often bear little resemblance to what companies pay for wood in a competitive market setting. This leads many people, including American trade and forest company officials, to conclude we are surrendering some of the world's finest softwood for a song. The Forest Renewal Plan takes a step in the right direction by increasing the stumpage charges levied companies cutting Crown timber. But in the months and years ahead, demand for softwood lumber will exceed supply, forcing prices up. With its new plan, government is securing added revenues for its coffers, but industry can now afford to pay more, way more. To underline this point, on the same day the Forest Renewal Plan was announced, shareholders attending MacMillan Bloedel Ltd.'s annual general meeting in Vancouver heard how despite anticipated increases in stumpage charges the company expected to post a threefold increase in earnings in 1994. This would suggest that we are likely to witness a continued relinquishment of BC's raw resources at less than true market value. This is economic surrender, and it spells trouble now and in the future.

The downward spiral

In his basement rec room in a suburban Victoria bungalow, Ray Travers, a professional forester turned forest policy consultant, sits surrounded by proof of the giveaway. Mounds of forest industry reports, filing boxes and papers spill across the floor. His desk is full to overflowing, and the computer on it is chirping away as if it wants his attention. A longtime participant in and observer of the forest industry, Travers has watched some very unsettling trends over the years, and he traces their origin to the early 1960s, when logging levels were a relatively modest 30 million cubic metres a year. He foresees economic disaster for the forest industry and the province, and he warms to his topic—the "downward spiral" of the volume economy—with an indignant passion.

"The implicit policy has been to make less with more," he says. "Industry and government may not have said that, but that's what's been happening, particularly since 1982 when there was a clear decision by the industry to replace labour with capital." Having made massive investments in machinery that

Can't cants be counted?

We're saying the same thing. What is the difference between taking a 12-inch round log and putting it on a ship and running it through a breakdown unit that takes four sides off, or shipping out a 11½ by 11½ cant? To us, it's the same thing. You haven't created any work within our province from our greatest resource.

Larry Rewalkowski, first vice-president, IWA–Canada, Local 1–85, quoted in *Report of Proceedings of the Select Standing Committee on Forests, Energy, Mines and Petroleum Resources* (Issue 8, Ladysmith, January 12, 1993).

After a massive worldwide buildup in commodity pulp production during the 1980s, pulp mills like this one in Campbell River have cut production to reduce inventories. And that's meant reduced employment for thousands of workers in the province's once-booming pulp and paper sector. Al Harvey photo.

displaced workers, industry then needed more "fibre" to justify its expenditures. "They applied to the government to do that, and they got it," Travers says. The problem is, much of this new machinery was designed to pump out a limited number of commodity products at a rapid rate. When markets were good this economic strategy worked well for the companies and their remaining workers. But when markets fell, workers and communities paid the price.

In this light, the productivity treadmill of our current forest economy emerges. With its growing capital investments, the industry needs huge volumes of resource throughput—trees—simply to break even and pay down its fixed costs. Once the break-even level is achieved, profits are made by processing additional quantities with a small incremental margin on each unit sold. Commodity prices rise and fall easily because the products are mass-produced, not distinctive, and there are plenty of competitors. When demand and prices rise as they did in 1993, mills operate at peak capacity churning through as many logs as possible. Such upturns in the market force commodity mills to retool to stay competitive. The end result: more throughput and less labour in each mill, and more industry consolidation as smaller mills give way to large. The overall trend is clear. Rather than creating more value with the wood and thereby more jobs, companies process more wood with less economic return and fewer jobs.

"We don't even do well with respect to the rest of Canada, which is just crazy," Travers says. "We start with the best timber in Canada and we log somewhere around half the volume for the entire country. We produce one-third the value of manufacturing shipments of forest products. And we generate 28

percent of the direct forest industry jobs. We start with the best and wind up with the least." This is what Travers means by the downward spiral.

Not a couple of miles away, another dissident forest consultant works away in his basement study. Mike Major is not a professional forester, but a log scaler who spent almost twenty years valuing BC's timber for private companies and the Ministry of Forests where he served as provincial scaling coordinator. Like Travers, Major is a man with a mission, his keen interest being the business of forestry: how trades are made, who sells wood to whom, and for how much. Notices of advertised and just-completed log sales pour out of his fax machine for immediate scrutiny. Attacking his subject with an almost frenetic enthusiasm, Major pinpoints what he sees to be the problem: a tenure system that shelters companies from a true market. Instead of having to compete for their wood on an open market, licence holders simply pay stumpage to the government, a fee Major says is far too low. "The idea of the tenure system is to get away from the idea of having a comparative value in the marketplace. The total objective of the tenure system is to turn each individual corporation into its own internal market," says Major.

It's no surprise, then, that sawmills owned by major tenure holders may actually subtract rather than add value to the logs they process. Under the present system, a log that could fetch $200 a cubic metre in a competitive market might be run through a mill and be turned into lumber worth $100 a cubic metre. The sawmilling company can argue it's added value, but only if the price it paid for the log was artificially set at $50, well below the true market value.

Major calls this value-subtracted. "Just imagine you're in South Africa. You're in a De Beers mine somewhere, and you come up with this diamond the size of your tape recorder. It's a beautiful diamond. It contains jewellery-grade diamond. And somebody says: `Who cares? We're not going to sell that one into Brussels to get converted into gem-quality stuff.' They take a hammer to it and say: `See, now we have tool bits. We got machine tool bits.' That's what we've done with our forests in British Columbia. We've brought it down to the lowest common denominator, the lowest economic standard."

Under such circumstances it becomes easy to understand why BC's valuable old-growth wood is shipped out of places like Stewart and Vancouver in virtually raw form for reprocessing south of the border, or in Japan. Companies can square a round log into a cant, say they've added value to it, and then ship it across the Canada–US border to Washington state where the real value is extracted. Or they can send whole logs and partially processed products to Japan where large pieces of wood are delivered in small, individual orders to labour-intensive mills that literally sculpt the wood into unique and costly finished products. In BC just the opposite happens. The province's wood manufacturing sector is geared to maximize profit through constantly increasing throughput. The end result is a profusion of low-value commodity products that, because of their sheer number, provide for handsome profits in good markets, and losses and worker layoffs when markets dry up.

Many analysts of BC's forest industry believe the historic undervaluing of our old-growth and the resulting low-value commodity-based manufacturing is proving to be a costly mistake. What the provincial government could have done long ago was learn how to capture the true value from the Crown's timber starting in the forest and ending in the mills. In the woods outside the tenures of the major corporations, there are many who see the costs of this failure every day. One is Herman Hans, an independent Prince Rupert logger and director of the Real Market Loggers' Association. The public, Hans says, isn't getting the best dollar for timber logged on Crown land. "We're letting that opportunity slip through our policies. And one of the cornerstones of our policy is the tenure system," Hans says.

Hauling logs through Williams Lake. Gary Fiegehen photo.

Concentrating The Cut

*Share of committed harvesting rights held
by 10 largest companies*

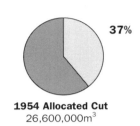

37%

1954 Allocated Cut
26,600,000m³

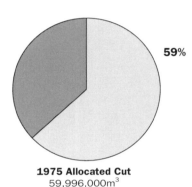

59%

1975 Allocated Cut
59,996,000m³

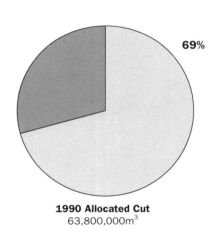

69%

1990 Allocated Cut
63,800,000m³

Source: Forest Resources Commission, The Future of
Our Forests *(1993).*

For Hans, the choice is clear. We can continue to watch some of the best softwood in the world leave the province in raw log or undermanufactured form. We can continue to accept artificially low domestic prices for wood and the poor forest management that results. Or we can change the tenure system and get more wood into an open, competitive setting where it commands a higher price, and adopt policies that create more logging and milling jobs.

"The companies who have the tenure, they aren't really creating any jobs," Hans says. "The economy takes a little dip, and they just lay off massive amounts of people. One of the reasons these same companies were given secure, long-term access to publicly owned timber in the first place was to provide sustained employment in smaller communities. The whole concept was we'll give you so much supply and on the other hand you create stable economies and communities by providing stable employment. But any time the economy takes a little dip those 150 people working in the sawmill, they get laid off. And whose responsibility do they become? The towns'."

In the end, Travers, Major and Hans offer similar assessments of trends in the BC forest economy. The increasing global scarcity of quality old-growth timber is creating luxury potential for BC, giving the province a distinct advantage in a world running short of precious natural resources. But corporate, government and union policies remain hooked on a volume economy of mass commodity production based on the logging and processing of old-growth timber that could be turned into some of the highest-value forest products in the world. As if in a process of reverse alchemy, we still convert our old-growth gold into the dull lead of commodity two-by-fours.

This is the mega-mill mentality that still blinds our big centralized institutions, the Carnaby mentality of corporate rationalization and back-room tenure deals. To Travers, this is the downward spiral; to Major it's value-subtracted. Whatever phrase is applied, one thing is certain: our old-growth inheritance is being rapidly squandered to the detriment of good economics and our natural environment.

To avoid the degraded future that awaits BC, we need a new approach to our old-growth. The challenge, says Professor David Cohen of the University of BC's School of Forestry, is to recognize the true value in what we have remaining, to learn from the mistakes of today before we have nothing left. Because it's the uniqueness of what we have now that gives us an advantage in a world running short of old-growth softwood. "I can remember when western red cedar was a junk species," Cohen recalls. "I was in the woods doing road layout and senior management personnel would look past the cedar to get to the spruce to promote plywood production. Today the same management personnel would dearly love to get that cedar which was eight foot in the butt, and the top log was absolutely clear. The spruce that was used as number-one peeler logs to produce sheathing, is now used to make guitar tops. Solid wood. High quality, high value, escalating prices. People will start to invest in wood just like they do with diamonds."

Instead the whole process of economic centralization robs BC of the value of its resource base. Almost all our wood is locked up in large corporate tenures, cut by ever fewer loggers and their big machines. And the whole system is managed by provincial officials who are often removed from the places or people their decisions affect. Local communities have no say, while small operators are allowed access to only a tiny fraction of the land base.

Dependence and surrender

Still, the forest industry in BC remains a vitally important part of our economy, one on which many individual communities and the province depend. To talk seriously about the future of BC's forests we must recognize the province's dependence on the forest industry and the change that looms before it. Environmental groups are quick to point to declining employment levels over the past decade as a sign of the industry's lack of commitment to forestry-dependent communities. But they incorrectly minimize our continuing dependence on the industry, and damage the credibility of the environmental message for politicians and policy makers as a result.

The job numbers, in fact, are still very high. In a background paper prepared for participants, the Commission on Resources and the Environment stated that in 1991 a "total of 272,100 people and their families" relied on BC's forest industry for their employment. CORE arrived at its number using a controversial industry multiplier of two indirect jobs for every direct job in the industry. But even if one disputes the multiplier chosen, there are a lot of jobs—high-wage jobs—at stake.

And the industry's importance, and our dependence on it, is even greater than these numbers reveal. Forest products account for about 45 percent of BC's manufacturing shipments. In 1993, the value of all manufactured shipments of BC forest products amounted to $13.8 billion. Moreover, forestry is itself very much an export-based industry. Over three-quarters of the industry's entire output is sold internationally—$6.5 billion, or 55 percent of the value of all forest products exports, to the United States alone. BC produces just under 30 percent of world softwood lumber exports; some even call it the world price setter in this commodity. These numbers point to significant job and business dependence. But government dependence is perhaps even greater. Just 1,000 cubic metres of wood (28 truckloads of logs) funnel almost $19,000 in resource royalties, income and corporate taxes into government coffers. With annual logging rates around 74 million cubic metres, it is sobering to contemplate just how deeply BC is attached to the welfare of the forest economy.

That is why all talk of changing direction must be carefully examined and publicly debated, particularly when the talk is initiated by companies who have laid off thousands of workers in the last decade. The Western Wood Products Forum is a body composed exclusively of senior executives of big forest companies such as Fletcher Challenge, MacMillan Bloedel and Canfor, and representatives from the IWA and the provincial and federal governments. In a 1992 study, the Forum noted that the industry's dependence on narrow international commodity markets, especially those in the US, meant that it had "tied itself very closely to demand cycles" and was thus highly vulnerable to "periods of market decline and recessions in the US." As a result, the Forum warned the provincial government that strategically, it "has a number of decisions to make," and it had better make them "quickly and beneficially" to their industry if the government is to "influence the level of private sector capital investment in British Columbia."

On this latter point, the report was blunt, even threatening: "Capital is highly mobile. Recent investments by British Columbia companies outside the province suggest that a positive investment climate in British Columbia will be an important precondition to achieving a successful `transition' to future prosperity." Under the existing conditions of dependence, these are the rules of the game. To the Forum, these rules translate into a specific strategic direction for both

---

Multiplying multipliers

In the Clayoquot Sound analysis, annual cutting rates were excessive, and both the regional and the provincial multipliers for non-direct employment were too high.

The analysis estimated that the base case supported 1,422 direct and non-direct forestry-related jobs regionally and 3,471 provincially. A more realistic estimate, based on a sustainable cutting rate and adjustments in the regional and provincial employment multipliers, indicates base camp employment of 839 direct and non-direct forestry-related jobs regionally and 1,744 provincially. The employment estimates in the analysis were high by 69% regionally and 99% provincially.

Trevor Jones, Critique of methods the BC Government uses to assess socio-economic implications of forestry/conservation strategies (consultant's report, January 1994).

industry and government. The industry needs to be assured by government of a continued access to a flow of wood, and it must position itself to meet the trade challenges of the emerging global economy.

At about the same time as the Forum made its views known, industry representatives from across Canada gathered under the white sails of the Vancouver Trade and Convention Centre for a convention dubbed Forest Summit '92. Summit participants looked at trends in the global market and future changes in wood supply (read less old-growth), and concluded BC would soon produce less solid wood products and much more particleboard, fibreboard and engineered wood products. It also concluded the demand for paper and paperboard products would almost double. To meet these projections, the Forest Summit report, *Rising to the Challenge!*, contemplated free trade, high technology, highly automated logging, the closure of uncompetitive pulp mills and the construction of new "world scale" mills. And to feed all these new capital-intensive, low-labour mills, the report called for the maintenance of a 90-million-cubic-metre-a-year logging rate—about 450,000 truckloads of wood per year above today's allowable annual cut.

This is big industry's blueprint for economic transition—a vision that pushes us down the same rocky road we've followed these many years. On this route, more workers will lose their jobs, more communities will suffer mill closures, more old-growth forests will be converted to plantations that will never yield the kind of wood products that have given BC its distinction in today's marketplace. Disturbing as this scenario is, it continues to have a profound influence on government. In this light, the refusal of the NDP government to change the tenure system that favours the very companies in question, is only to be expected. As then Aboriginal Affairs Minister Andrew Petter told a province-wide CORE meeting, "the constraints of current capital markets" make it difficult, if not impossible, to change the course we're on without risking international financing repercussions.

Conflict rising

These constraints are, in all likelihood, the biggest obstacles to overcome if we are to change our forest-based volume economy. For that is what has driven the employment and environmental trends of the last few years. Whether it is the Council of Forest Industries of BC, the Ministry of Forests, or the IWA–Canada, control of BC's forests and their economic future is dominated by the specific interests of big centralized corporate, governmental and union institutions. And often the lines between the three camps blur, with senior officials moving from one job in one camp to a high-profile job in another. Ken Drushka, a writer and forestry critic, observes that the forest industry in BC "has evolved into a form of organization that could be called monopoly corporatism." The large corporations that dominate the industry in BC have eliminated competition. "They do not sell their timber on an open market where it would be available to ever more efficient mills, and they are the major threat to the remaining vestiges of a resident business community. On a provincial level, they, their unions and the Ministry of Forests constitute a single monolithic entity."

This power structure now presides over its own demise. Labour unions

Moving elsewhere

There is nothing to prevent internationalized companies from moving elsewhere. Since they have relatively little stake in the communities where their plants are located, and alternative fibre sources elsewhere, it might well be in their interests to cut BC's forests at a rapid pace while there remains markets for logs and pulp....The value of BC trees could increase substantially on a market for specialty products, but that would require selective logging, more intensive silviculture and thinning, and re-designed manufacturing plants.

M. Patricia Marchak, "Global Markets in Forest Products: Sociological Impacts on Kyoto Prefecture and British Columbia Interior Forest Regions" (Paper prepared for *Journal of Business Administration*, special edition on forestry management policy, 1989).

Cross-fertilization

Jack Munro (left). Before: President of International Woodworkers of America. After: Chairman of the industry-funded Forest Alliance of BC.
Claude Richmond (centre). Before: Minister of Forests. After: Chairman of the Western Environment and Development Task Force, a forest industry lobby group at the Rio Earth Summit.
Mike Apsey (right). Before: Deputy Minister of Forests. After: President of the Council of Forest Industries of BC, the province's pre-eminent industry association.

continue to lose members at dizzying rates. The cut available to corporate tenure holders slides ever downward. And the government's financial position, so closely linked to individual and corporate taxes in the forest industry, continues to worsen with a $26.4-billion debt and an annual billion-dollar-plus deficit. Yet in the face of this inexorable decline, there's little to indicate that those at the top are willing even to contemplate change. They continue to subsist on a model of economic growth and development that demands a continuous flow of resource wealth out of the frontier. This volume-oriented approach is maladapted to the needs of a sustainable future, but it is fiercely resistant to change. New governments that promise change instead become mere new managers of the same old processes.

As environmentalist Sile Simpson and logger Herman Hans attest, challenging this structure is not easy. But rarely do the problems rise to the prominent public heights of a Carmanah or Clayoquot Sound. Usually they just simmer away at the local level where no one hears about them, and frustration prevails. These conflicts will not be resolved by setting aside 12 or even 15 percent of the land base, for the issue is broader than wilderness protection. Indeed, whether it's in the north, the Cariboo, the Kootenays or the coastal Gulf Islands, whether among Natives or non-Natives, the conflict with the old volume economy is everywhere. An acrimony infects the province. To expel it we must focus on the economic causes underlying it, and on the economic transition on which all else depends.

But it seems we are incapable of making this transition, so the conflict spreads. Munro and Moore may disagree with McCrory's "Brazil of the North," but the label sticks. For years, BC has been getting bad press internationally—the *New Yorker, Die Zeit,* the *Observer.* But the threat has escalated in recent years. The target is clear—foreign buyers don't like how BC treats the forests from whence they buy their wood. Jean Jeanrenaud, the forests campaigner for the Worldwide Fund for Nature (WWF) in London, England, is blunt: "There is a

Ecosystems first

Ecological sustainability must...be the cornerstone of the proposed new Forest Practices Act. We appreciate that the government has taken some positive steps in this direction through some regional timber harvesting guidelines that endeavour to protect biodiversity. However, it is evident that forests are still predominantly viewed as a source of fibre supply, and so far guidelines to protect biodiversity do little more than pay lip service to the need to maintain non-timber values. Sadly, the Code does little if anything to remedy this situation.

Sierra Club of Western Canada, Victoria, Comments on the Forest Practices Code (December 1993).

Economics first

Heritage, cultural, wildlife, recreation and other values are important, do provide benefits, and deserve to be taken seriously in forest management policy. But the province's *economic and social* needs cannot be overlooked. Implementation of the Forest Practices Code as currently envisaged would have a major impact on the rate of harvesting of British Columbia's timber resources, which in turn would affect jobs, investment tax revenues, and the economic base of many communities....

Business Council of British Columbia, Comments on the Proposed Forest Practices Code (December 1993).

Canada's Endangered Forests

TIME

Who A

CHINA DAILY

Saturday, October 30, 1993   Price 30 fen, 35 fen airmail

Vol. 13 No. 3900

Opponents dig in for forest battle

THE OBSERVER

Bloc Bookings   Scorsese's women   Serious money   England's big test

Environment

Canada's Troubled Trees

Environmentalists fight both Ottawa and a giant industry to protect ancient forests

San Francisco Chronicle

THE LARGEST DAILY CIRCULATION IN NORTHERN CALIFORNIA

Price $1.75   77-11

MONDAY, JULY 19, 1993

Canada's Endangered Rain Forests

May 14, 1990

THE NEW YORKER

50,

DER SPIEGEL

Plünderer im Norden

Nicht nur in den Tropen stirbt der Wald. Fast unbemerkt von der Öffentlichkeit verschwinden auch die letzten Urwälder der Nordhalbkugel durch großflächigen Raubbau. Bei Kahlschlägen in Kanada und Finnland, Alaska und Sibirien fallen jahrhundertealte Bäume, die als Rohstoff für Windeln und Werbebroschüren enden.

Ich riskiere meine Existenz", sagt Anja Finne, 49, Oberförsterin im finnischen Bezirk Kainuu, „aber soll ich unsere letzten Wildniswälder den Bulldozern überlassen?"
Försterin Finne kämpft ... nen Amtsstuben ge...
Die mächti...
Finn...

Mit ungewohnter Heftigkeit prallen im ... nd der vermeint-... Land der 50 00... älder (auf jeden lich un... ...ar) die Interes-... ...alle Welt um ... ...bangt", sagt ... in Helsinki. ... ...hunderteal-... ...g umgelegt, mit ... Umwelt sind ... ...g weniger schlimm tur Entrindet, gehackseh ... kocht, enden t... nen a...

zwar mit Treibhaus-Setzlingen bestückt, doch die neuen Holzplantagen, so Forstwirtin Kuvaja, „machen noch lange keinen Wald aus".
„Don't finnish the forests" – mit diesem Slogan wollen die Greenpeacer die Not der „borealen" (Boreas: griech. ... fur „Nordwind") Wälder... punkt rücken...

Manchester Guardian Weekly

growing dissatisfaction with the way the Canadian government, and the BC government in particular, have dealt with the issues. The BC government appears to be nothing but a puppet for the industry." These concerns, he says, could be disaster for BC: "It's an assault on the entire industry."

A future beyond

Despite the fires of conflict that rage across the province and around the world, a consensus lies beneath the surface of apparent disparity, waiting to sprout like fireweeds after the blaze has passed. The various initiatives launched by the government—the Forest Renewal Act, the Protected Areas Strategy, CORE, the Biodiversity Guidelines, the Forest Practices Act—are partial solutions, and they are a necessary and important beginning. But the deeper challenge lies ahead, in the economic realm where we can move beyond the twin subsidies of environmental and community decline that underpin our volume economy. As we shall see, a range of new businesses and community initiatives reveal a willingness to think anew about our future, to begin the move to an upward spiral. But still the trends of the status quo are downward, toward industry rationalization, unemployment, community erosion, biological impoverishment and economic surrender.

To avoid being projected into this future, we must envision another one, and make it happen.

CHAPTER FIVE

THE NEW FOREST ECONOMY

I T IS A WARM, SUNNY LATE AUTUMN MORNING IN THE YEAR 2005. Delegates to the fifth annual Interior Eco-Forestry Convention spill onto a large patio outside the stunning timber-frame trade and convention centre at Big White ski resort near Kelowna. Jim Smith has just delivered a talk on how a log market near Lumby, a wildly successful venture initiated by the Ministry of Forests a dozen years earlier in 1993, is now widely employed by communities throughout BC as a means of generating higher timber-cutting revenues and better forest practices. Now, in need of some fresh air, Smith strolls to the end of the patio and looks across the valley to the scarred hillsides of Grano Creek. He is soon joined by Loni Parker, a longtime member of the Revelstoke Forest Corporation's board of directors and Keith Wyton, president of Sarita Furniture Ltd., Port Alberni's biggest furniture manufacturer.

"I wonder whether we'd even be here today if that kind of logging had been allowed to continue," Smith says as he gazes at the distant devastated landscape. Parker and Wyton murmur assent, but are quickly lost in talk about how credit unions are clamouring to joint-venture with community forestry boards on local value-added milling projects. Before long, the convention coordinator, a former Forests Minister, calls the delegates back inside for the day's last two sessions—a look at how BC's completed parks and wilderness system is credited with tripling tourist visits to the province since 1995, and a panel discussion on how BC's burgeoning army of woodlot owners are profiting from the regional log yards where they market and sell their timber. Convention 2005 will end that evening with a banquet for more than 500 guests.

That month, a quick survey of headlines around the province reveals a very different British Columbia than the conflict-ridden landscape of only a dozen years before. Just a few weeks earlier, the *Cariboo Observer* trumpeted: "Horse Loggers' Jamboree Draws 2,000 Contestants." The business section of the *Vancouver Sun* reported that "Credit Union Financing of Remanufacturing hits $5 billion," and that a new form of "System Tourism Peaks at 200,000 Visitors." (System tourism, it seems, refers to a new province-wide travel package of coastal kayaking and mountain touring, much in demand by visiting Europeans.)

Opposite: Unlogged forest near Keremeos in BC's southern interior. Al Harvey photo.

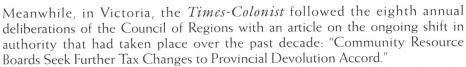

Meanwhile, in Victoria, the *Times-Colonist* followed the eighth annual deliberations of the Council of Regions with an article on the ongoing shift in authority that had taken place over the past decade: "Community Resource Boards Seek Further Tax Changes to Provincial Devolution Accord."

Changes in the landscape are also evident in the way people live. Over the past decade, a broad wood culture has emerged in the province. Showcasing local wood is all the rage in commercial buildings: timbered beams and laminated trusses are overtaking the drab steel and concrete boxes so fashionable in the latter decades of the twentieth century. On shop walls and in people's homes, the soft warmth of finished cedar and fir has gradually replaced the gyproc and cold metals of the past. In universities and offices, sustainable forestry is now conventional wisdom, and it is fuelling a renaissance in local production and use of wood products. Provincial exports are booming to markets that insist on sustainable production. Everywhere people are demanding the world class craftsmanship evident in British Columbia's finished wood products. In 2005, a new forest economy is taking root, and everywhere, small businesses are prospering. In the process, those who were once sworn enemies—the environmentalist and the logger, the tourist operator and the logging company—have become allies in a new era of prosperity and sustainability.

Back from the future

A fantasy? A Forestopia? Yes. But an impossibility? No. This is our vision, and it is a vision shared by many others who look to a different future for British Columbia's rich and diverse forests. In the 1990s, imagining alternative futures has become very popular in small communities and government commissions alike. People are clearly anxious to resolve the conflicts of the decade. Trying to envision a different future underlies much of the appeal of "sustainable development." But the phrase itself, and the processes undertaken in its name, are slippery. In the absence of some agreement on what sustainable development actually is, the signal outcome of the sustainability debate has been a fad for "process"—if we only talk enough, rational people and good intentions will prevail.

In the late 1980s and early 1990s that fad translated into a host of round-table discussions, consensus negotiations, stakeholder forums and mediation techniques. But the end product was almost always the same: a collection of vague generalities on which everyone could agree because they provided no one with any real guidance. On the specifics, the stalemate lingered. The Clayoquot and Carnaby conflicts raged on, off limits to consensus because some vested interest disagreed. And while the talking continued, the vision actually being pursued went on the same. Business-as-usual pressed on; the future was merely the present forecast ahead.

One person who specializes in "visioning" is John Robinson, Director of the University of British Columbia's new Sustainable Development Research Institute. "The future isn't out there as a juggernaut coming on us that we have to respond to, that we can predict and therefore react to," he says. "The future will be what it is because of what we do today. So our actions are, in part, creating that future. And that means that issues about the future have to do with choice."

"We're always wrong, always wrong, when we try and predict the future," Robinson told delegates attending a CORE meeting in Richmond in the late spring of 1993. Like other panelists attending the workshop, Robinson was there to talk about the socioeconomic implications of various land-use options then being considered by the commission. But he argued that the starting point for discussion should not be forecasting what these changes would mean, but looking at what people wanted for the future and backcasting from that vision to

---

Radically different economics

As the term "sustainable development" has been embraced by the political mainstream, so it has been stripped of its original concern with ensuring future ecological stability. It is no longer a challenge to the conventional economic paradigm but rather has become another excuse for continued economic growth. True sustainability demands a radically different economics which fully recognizes the processes and limits of the biosphere.

William Rees, "The Ecology of Sustainable Development," in *The Ecologist* (Vol. 20, No. 1, 1990).

identify the changes needed now to get there. "What we don't want to know, particularly, is what's the most likely future," Robinson said. "It's probably one we don't want. What we want to know more about is what else there is out there. And what we could have if we made the right decisions. That's an interesting question. The key then is not what's most likely, but what else could be. And how do we decide what could be. The focus shifts to desirable futures rather than likely futures."

If we are no longer content merely to extrapolate, or forecast our future from the present, then the whole reference point of public debate changes. Backcasting from a new vision of a value economy offers an alternative, filling the vacuum left by the demise of the old jobs-versus-environment controversies. No longer need we freeze at the question "How many jobs will it cost?" and then keep on cutting. Instead, we can openly ask: "What kind of industry might actually sustain us? What can we do now to get there?" Whatever side one might be on, here, at least, the real debate is joined.

In looking to the future, however, a detailed plan or a draft Utopia is not what is needed. The world is too dynamic and too chaotic for that. But to escape the empty platitudes of much of the current debate, we must look at how our unsustainable institutions work today, and what sustainable alternatives might entail. As we have argued at the beginning of this book, at stake in our forest conflict is the difficult shift from a volume to a value economy. To address this shift seriously has been, and remains, off limits because it questions the current corporate model. How do we get the very institutions that embody our grow-and-conquer compulsions to create an alternative?

Forestopia—and how to get it

Grant Copeland, a New Denver environmentalist and economic consultant, sees this contradiction every day. He just needs to look at the line of blacktop running by town and through the scenic Slocan Valley. He and his colleagues in the Valhalla Society are fighting for the few pockets of wilderness remaining in the region, while the province spends millions of dollars to upgrade the road—an upgrade many local residents believe is for the benefit of one form of traffic: chip trucks bound for the expanded Celgar pulp mill in nearby Castlegar. The same holds true for a new $26-million bridge across the Columbia River, a bridge that will cut travel time to the mill, which doubled its output in 1993. There is economic growth here, but linear growth which fuels an expanded mill that creates few if any new jobs, and at a time when regional forest resources are dwindling.

"What we need is a fundamental change in the way we approach economic development," says Copeland. "We need to figure out where we can really go with economic development that is environmentally sustainable, socially acceptable and economically feasible. And we're not doing that right now. We're supporting mega-projects and maintaining the status quo interests of large multinational corporations, particularly with regard to the forest industry."

Thus does Celgar increase its production, expecting sales volumes to increase; workers go further into debt, anticipating future wage hikes; governments approve unsustainable cut levels and spend more money on inappropriate infrastructure, hoping to keep it all afloat. In the end our existing economic model actually exaggerates the hardship of resource depletion because it can function only with more flow, fewer jobs and continued growth. With growth an end in itself, we fail to examine the direction of our economy, to distinguish healthy from unhealthy growth.

Imagining healthy growth in practical terms is not a difficult exercise. As we have seen, the processes underlying the volume economy are extractive and

Falling rain

The language of commerce sounds specific, but in fact it is not explicit enough. If Hawaiians had 138 different ways to describe falling rain, we can assume that rain had an profound importance in their lives. Business, on the other hand, only has two words for profit—gross and net. The extraordinarily complex manner in which a company recovers profit is reduced to a single numerically neat and precise concept. It makes no distinctions as to how the profit was made. It does not factor in whether people or places were exploited, resources depleted, communities enhanced, lives lost, or whether the entire executive suite was in such turmoil as to require stress consultants and outplacement services for the victims. In other words, business does not discern whether the profit is one of quality, or mere quantity.

Paul Hawken, *The Ecology of Commerce* (New York: HarperCollins, 1993).

A sailboat crew and kayakers cruise by the Queen Charlotte Islands' temperate rain forest. Alan Etkin photo.

linear—getting the wood out from one place to supply bigger mills someplace else. To sustain our social organization, which is addicted to this linear growth, the volume economy achieves its wealth by sapping communities and environments of theirs. The value economy, in contrast, assumes that ecological and community processes are circular. That is, to be sustainable, these processes must maintain themselves, living on the stock of natural and social capital with which they have been endowed, so that they can return long-term stability to the forest and long-term value to the local community.

This is Forestopia, a time and place that takes its sustenance from an economy that returns health, not injury, to the environment and the community. Forests are allowed their diversity of trees, shrubs, mosses, lichens, hundreds of species of animals and millions of subsoil organisms, each of which is important to the others in ways that are just beginning to be understood. Big old trees, large dead snags, downed logs on the ground and in streams play multiple roles in maintaining a healthy environment. Reductionist forestry techniques such as clearcutting and slash-burning sacrifice this principle. And when we take a linear, extractive, single-interest, one-way approach to the forest, we compromise the strength of its complex whole, and we create serious structural problems. When the forest is removed or burned, there are too few big trees left to shade soils and new growth from excessive heat, to offer nesting habitat for birds, to establish stream breaks for spawning salmon or their juvenile offspring, to give shelter to small animals, to buffer the land against wind and water erosion, to provide nutrients for new growth. To hope to retain our vast forest heritage, we must reduce the linear, one-way flow out of the forest, and we must do so across the entire landscape.

If ecology is the foundation of natural relations, community is the

A different forest paradigm

We would like to propose a different forest paradigm. We believe that foresters should strive to manage forests so as to maintain the processes that characterize natural forest ecosystems. Towards this objective, the goal of management activities is to maintain, protect, and where necessary, to create natural forest structures. Logging is permitted only to the extent and in a manner that it does not impair ecological processes or environmental assets. This system does not promise an even flow of wood products form the forests. The efficacy of silvicultural practices is evaluated by biological rather than market-based criteria.

US Forest Service technical report, cited in Natural Resource Defense Council Memorandum "Summary of Issues Related to the Recent California Spotted Owl Decision" (San Francisco, January 21, 1993).

foundation of social relations, and requires equally careful attention. What is community and how does it work? What are the forces that threaten to undermine it? These are questions people like Graham Morgan and Mark Brett spend a lot of time thinking about, thanks to the corporate plans that have put so many people in their communities out of work. The volume economy has undermined the health of their human communities as profoundly as it has the environment. In contrast, the value economy depends on the strength of its local character. Just as healthy ecosystems recirculate nutrients and water locally, so too a healthy community economy is internally dynamic, recirculating wealth locally in a diversified economy that is only partly dependent on outside employers and outside markets. A tree that is cut on the woodlot, milled by a sawyer, sold to a local furniture maker, whose product is then purchased by the doctor in town or the farmer up the valley, is very different from a tree that is cut or pulped and shipped directly to Japan. The key to all this is that a healthy economy can draw on both linear and circular processes in a balanced way: local resources generating exports and local resources generating local returns.

How can we achieve this healthy, diverse economy, so unlike the contemporary single-industry town in the volume economy? By recognizing the real costs and limits to growth, the new value economy accepts that some kinds of economic activity will decline while others grow. It provides a new model of economic development, a model that requires three dimensions of change.

Three Dimensions of Change
Volume to Value

Value-added. The phrase has the ring of truth that nobody can deny. That's why in the last few years the concept has gone from obscurity to cliché. But what does it mean? If you wrap a stack of wood in plastic, does that add value? If you lull an overseas buyer with advertisements that your product comes from Forests Forever, does that add value? To some, the answer is yes: higher market share and profits are the only "values" that count. To others, "value" has more substance.

The first dimension of change is the need to shift from a volume-based economy of mass production to a value-oriented industry of specialized product. This doesn't mean we lose every highly mechanized primary lumber mill and pulp mill now dotting the landscape, far from it. But we need to move quickly to solve the clear overcommitment/undersupply problem facing us. We simply have too much productive capacity given our shrinking forest land base. To protect ecological values we must bring the volume down, way down, below the levels currently bandied about. And the only way we can offset that reduction is to bring up, way up, the value extracted from the wood that we do cut. In other words, for each cubic metre of wood processed there must be greater social and financial returns to local communities and the province as a whole.

Working with wood. Kitselas band members building log home near Terrace. Myron Kozak photo.

Capital to Labour

Accompanying the move from volume to value is a second dimension of change: moving from capital- to labour-based activities. In the volume economy, it is almost a law of nature that success depends on shedding labour. The

MacMillan Bloedels of this world can ignore the social erosion that results, because it is not in their success equation. But communities do so at their own peril. Ironically, the forest industry that publicly justifies itself with inflated employment multipliers seeks to reduce them through its capital-intensive productivity strategy. In contrast, the value economy maximizes the impact of the multiplier effect by designing its production system around diverse, locally based, labour-intensive industries. This is what the so-called new competition is all about.

The shift from labour to capital takes many forms, beginning in the forest.

For more than forty years Fred Linde has run a small custom-cut sawmill near Williams Lake. Unlike the large commodity sawmillers in town, Linde and his workers turn out a wide array of cut-to-order products, most for local customers. Much of the mill's labour-intensive production results in the output of tongue-and-groove panel boards, seen here. The mill cuts poplar, fir, pine and birch logs into valuable shelving stock, flooring and panelling. The whole operation is value-driven. "We wouldn't be here otherwise," Linde says.
Gary Fiegehen photo.

Take, for example, a contractor to a major forest company who invests in new state-of-the-art logging equipment. Suddenly, the contractor doesn't need as many people to haul logs out of the bush each day, but he's forced to work harder still. "Somebody talks him into buying a half-million-dollar feller buncher," says Jim Smith, a Vernon forester. "He's not employing any more people, but he's producing a lot more. And the money that he's generating is going to pay off that capital investment rather than paying wages. There's a cost, a social cost, to those kinds of machines. The cost is we're paying more unemployment benefits. There's a lot of hidden costs to that kind of mentality."

There are other profound human costs, costs that can't be measured in dollars and cents. And it's time we started talking a lot more about them. "Our society thinks of loggers as sort of dumb people," Smith says. "But most that I know are intelligent. They like working outdoors. They've got wives and kids. To me it's more important to provide them jobs rather than put the wood into the mill dirt cheap. And I'll tell you, the happiest loggers I know are the small loggers. The guys with a bit of equipment are a lot happier, more easy-going, more proud of what they do than the guys with the feller bunchers. Those guys are harried, hassled, running around with their heads cut off."

As we will see in the next chapter, there are lots of ways to put more people back to work in the woods. Yet our major resource industry continues to shed labour at an alarming rate while other sectors of the economy—especially services, wholesale and retail trade, food and accommodation—add jobs. Indeed, certain sectors of the forest industry—especially small business—are doing so too. And some of the excellent work already taking place in this area is the subject of Chapter 8. The shift from capital to labour means moving away from investments of more capital into costly, job-displacing, environment-consuming equipment that directs returns into remote corporations and governments. To move toward value means creating distinctive products that are job-intensive and resource-efficient, and that direct financial returns into the community. What matters is the character of the product, and that means how, and by whom, it is produced.

Corporate to Community

Reducing the volume but creating more jobs through new value-based small businesses has obvious appeal. In theory, at least, it meets every objective— environmental, social and economic. Certainly there are obstacles to be overcome. A worker laid off from the green chain at a large mill often cannot find replacement work in new value-added industries that depend on a more highly skilled, flexible workforce. Unionized mills also pay high wages that are difficult for small businesses to match, although the value-added wood manufacturing sector still provides good average wages. And displaced workers need job opportunities in their home communities. New value-added industries in the Lower Mainland are of little value to laid-off workers living throughout rural BC.

These challenges can be met if we move our economy away from its top-heavy corporate form, whether private or public, and invigorate new businesses and management authority in the local community. This is the third dimension of change we need in our pursuit of Forestopia, the move from corporate to community-based development strategies. In the pages that follow are examples of dynamic community industries that dominate the landscape, industries that are light on their feet in meeting the demands of a changing marketplace.

The new competition

The American [and Canadian] business enterprise and regulatory framework tend to be organized according to, or derived from, the principles of Big Business. The task is to make a transition to business and regulatory institutions organized in terms of the New Competition....The message that we are living in a time of economic transformation is not lost on managers and workers. Nevertheless progress is slow. The biggest barrier is social: transforming a way of industrial life....Small firms can be technologically advanced, generate high income jobs, and produce internationally competitive goods and services....Small firms in the United States are spearheading a process of continuous economic transformation.

Michael Best, *The New Competition: Institutions of Industrial Restructuring* (Cambridge MA: Harvard University Press, 1991).

The nature of community

The small community has historically been the most efficient at using energy, recycling its wastes, reducing drawdown, and adjusting to carrying capacity. A kind of unconscious wisdom operates at that level, I would argue, that is not necessarily available at other scales: the sensors of the society are most receptive, the feedback systems and information loops most effective, the decision-making mechanisms most adaptive and competent. This is the level, too, at which people have been shown to solve social problems most harmoniously, to survive randomness and change most easily, to know the maximum number of people with some intimacy, and to retain a sense of the self-amid-others most lugubriously. It is not by accident or devine decree, after all, that the limited community has lasted all these millennia. It is because it was *experientially* the most effective form for survival.

Kirkpatrick Sale, *Dwellers in the Land: The Bioregional Vision* (San Francisco: Sierra Club Books, 1985).

CHAPTER SIX

A BUSINESS OF STEWARDSHIP

L AST FALL FIVE MEN STARTED LOGGING ON A SLOPE ABOVE A scenic valley near Cherryville, a small farming community off Highway 6 between Vernon and Nakusp. The 8-kilometre-long valley bottom is blessed with good farmland. Many area residents make their living harvesting hay and raising livestock. For years, local residents fought tooth and nail against clearcutting the surrounding slopes for fear of damage to their water supplies. "We've had some real knockdown, drag 'em out battles over resource management here," says Hank Cameron, a local forest technician.

Into this hornet's nest walked Jim Smith, a resource officer for small business at the Ministry of Forests district office in Vernon. Smith too had a logging plan, but one with a difference. Instead of the clearcutting typical of the surrounding Arrow Lakes and Okanagan forest districts, Smith proposed a technique called strip selection logging in narrow bands of 15 to 20 metres across with 60-metre-wide buffers left in between to mask the cut. To get approval, Smith met with members of the Informed Cherryville Area Residents for the Environment, and in consultation with residents devised the specifics of his plan. "It's an important view shed and it's also part of a deer winter range," Smith said. But many of the trees also had root rot, and limited logging would clear out the diseased trees to make way for healthy new growth.

Smith got the requisite approvals and a short while later the logging began. It took the five-man crew consisting of one faller, two skidder operators, a bucker and one backhoe operator seven weeks to log about 2,660 cubic metres or 74 truckloads of wood off the hillside. When all the strips were added up, the total area logged amounted to a little under 8 hectares. Aside from the obvious appeal of a system that didn't leave a devastated landscape behind, this logging also had tremendous social benefits. Had the same land area been conventionally logged, the wood would have come out far more quickly with fewer people working. "If it was conventionally clearcut with a feller buncher it would have taken less than two weeks, easily less than two weeks," Smith says, adding the conventional system would employ no more than four people. "Who's getting the benefits of that? Who benefits? Just a handful of people."

When the logging finished, Smith drove up from his office in Vernon to snap some photographs of the hillside. As he stood by the side of the road some boys and girls rode up on horseback and asked him what he was doing. "I said: 'Hey! I'd like to get a picture of you looking at the logging.' And they looked at

Not like natural processes

One of the things we've tended to do in talking about forestry is persist in representing things like clear-cutting and broadcast burning as being similar to natural processes. This is not an accurate portrayal. It's not the way Nature does it at all; never was. Although clear-cutting may be a very effective way of accomplishing some of our objectives, it's just not the way Nature perpetuates ecosystems.

Jerry Franklin, "Old-Growth Forests and the New Forestry," in "Forests Wild and Managed: Differences and Consequences" (Symposium notes, University of British Columbia, January 19–20, 1990).

Opposite: Horse logger Roger Losier and partner in a stand of young conifers near Smithers. Myron Kozak photo.

the hillside and they said: `There isn't any logging.'" Smith then pointed up the slope to some barely perceptible cuts across the face. "Hey we like that a lot better than clearcutting," Smith recalls the children saying. "And I thought: `Right on you kids.'"

The Cherryville example is just one of many similar stories Smith has. It's easy to put many more people to work in the woods doing good logging, says Smith. Except for one impediment—broad mechanical clearcutting fits with the fibre requirements of an industry dominated by big companies, big mills and big appetites. No matter how promising the alternatives appear, they get lost in the frantic rush to get access to as many trees as possible.

Shifting the balance

Finding more wood obsesses forest planners. It is the topic of countless expert reports that often make for pretty scary reading. For example, a 1990 joint federal–provincial study entitled "Increasing the Utilization Level of British Columbia's Timber Harvest" envisions a vast expansion of the current liquidation regime into hitherto marginal stands—in other words, into landscapes that have so far been spared the feller bunchers because they were not considered "economic." This new interest has, in part, sped up with the development of new composite wood products—the particleboards and oriented strand boards which have opened up for chipping hardwood forests of aspen, birch, poplar and alder, as well as "decadent" stands of hemlock and balsam. But it's also driven by the inexorable clearcut march out of the accessible valley-bottom forests into higher, more remote stands of smaller trees.

In the study, the technocratic language of forest liquidation is bland, but the message is not. The industry, it says, "will move to develop, of its own volition, the orderly increased use of the standing timber available to it [which] would also have the advantage of allowing a replacement of decadent stands with thrifty new forests." Almost a battle cry to the industry, the study concludes: "It is once more to the frontier for the industry: `marginal wood' must and will be radically redefined in the 1990s."

While the industry is pushed out to the most distant margins of the old-growth forest, still other studies proliferate on the potential of the so-called thrifty new forests that will spring up once the old-growth overburden has been pushed aside. Here too some scary optimism awaits us. A 1989 BC Science Council report anticipated such intensive plantation production that, with sufficient investment, the potential yield would increase by 50 percent and the annual cut to 120 million cubic metres by the year 2020. While the NDP's Forest Renewal Plan avoids the use of such optimistic predictions, the plan was drafted with such optimism in mind. Certainly, its aim is to ensure that in today's volume economy as much wood as possible flows to the industry. Undoubtedly, without the Plan there will be a decline in logging rates as the government reviews timber supplies and names new parks. But with the Forest Renewal Plan in place, logging rates won't necessarily fall too fast or far. Indeed, the report posited that anticipated reductions in logging could be offset by the Plan, and that future logging levels could be even higher than today. "Some analysts suggest that it will only be possible to reverse, with a delay of several decades part of the drop," the Plan said. "Others believe that by taking appropriate steps now, future harvest levels can be higher than current levels, and short-term declines can be largely avoided."

"Others" include groups such as the Truck Loggers' Association, which concluded in a study of Vancouver Island's Strathcona Timber Supply Area that a 91 percent increase in yield could be achieved over the next century.

In practice, however, the silvicultural investment made to achieve even a

Stacking logs at a woodlot landing north of Quesnel. Ralph Currie photo.

shadow of this mechanically Orwellian utopia is abysmally low. Even the most basic silvicultural investment like tree planting, for example, has only been a legally mandated company responsibility since 1987. Meanwhile, enhanced or incremental silviculture—the spacing, thinning and pruning of trees—has not been required and is rarely done, even though it provides additional fibre to sawmills and improves the growing potential and quality of the remaining trees. Any change here runs up against the natural momentum of the volume economy. For one thing, companies argue that under the present tenure system there isn't the long-term security required to ensure they will have access to the trees they've made investments in. For another, industry profits are precarious and long-term investments in silviculture must compete with more immediate investments in equipment, roads and the transportation necessary to get at the timber. As one recent study put it, in the current system, "the production of timber to feed corporate conversion mills is regarded as an activity which generates costs rather than profits." Thus the costs of logging, let alone regeneration, are to be minimized as companies "only undertake those projects which reach or exceed a target rate of return on invested capital." In the volume economy, to act otherwise isn't "rational."

Under such conditions, how is it feasible for old-growth liquidation to be slowed, and a shift to forest tending made? Part of the answer lies on the other side of the equation, in new mills that use less wood and add more value. But in the woods too, value can be added and jobs created from fewer trees. And it can be done economically while logging fewer trees than in traditional clearcutting methods. To do this, we must treat our old-growth diamonds less like drill bits and more like jewels. At the same time, we must also start to nurture the underutilized second-growth we already have, taking out commercial wood now, while pruning the remaining trees to get the highest value from them years down the road. To its great credit, this is the central thrust of the Forest Renewal Plan.

Finding value where none was found before

In Sweden and Finland, there is virtually no commercial old-growth left, and the environment there is seriously degraded. Only two wild salmon-bearing runs remain, and wildlife habitat has been eroded with the countless marshes that were drained to create new tree farms. The present trajectory in BC is toward a similarly degraded fate. But it can still be avoided, if we learn what the Swedes were forced to learn by necessity. During the years after World War Two as BC's assault on its old-growth forests shifted into high gear, Sweden's natural forest was already largely exhausted. So the country turned its attention to cultivating a new forest instead. By extensive planting, thinning and fertilizing, Swedish yields increased dramatically to a point where today its sustained yield exceeds BC's by almost 50 percent. Sweden's so-called long-run sustained yield is estimated at 90 million cubic metres per year while BC's is only 59 million cubic metres, and that number may well drop further as various recalculations are done in timber supply areas and tree farm licences across BC. Yet Sweden's actual logging level is only 67 million cubic metres, while BC has greatly exceeded that cut, reaching as high as 90 million cubic metres. And BC's cut, it must be remembered, is almost completely old-growth, while fully one quarter of Sweden's annual cut comes from thinnings alone.

Many of the techniques employed in Scandinavia could be used here. With greater attention paid to retaining our old-growth by logging in a more selective fashion, we could avoid some of the environmental degradation and biological loss that characterizes Scandinavia's forests. Learning from the Swedes and Finns may also prove critical to bridging what the Truck Loggers' Association calls a looming "sawlog availability gap." As a recent paper penned under the co-operative Forest Resource Development Agreement recognized, the traditional supply of clear lumber from BC's old-growth forests is diminishing with a "corresponding increase in the premium value of clear lumber from second-growth stands." If industry is to be profitable in the future it is timely to recognize a simple fact: tended timber, particularly if it is pruned, is significantly more valuable than untended timber because it produces more of the old-growth characteristics of better appearance and larger dimensions of clear, knot-free wood.

Someone who appreciates this fact is Ken Drushka, a longtime forest critic and author. Using briefing documents supplied to the last Royal Commission on forestry in BC along with various Ministry of Forests timber and range inventories, Drushka has estimated just how big and valuable our second-growth forests are, particularly on the mainland coast, Vancouver Island and the Queen Charlottes where climatic conditions allow for big tree growth. His figure: about 500,000 hectares of commercially accessible forest between 40 and 120 years of age.

In one forty-year-old second-growth stand near Campbell River, Drushka reports, loggers did a commercial thinning, logging some of the standing timber while leaving the remaining trees to grow. The average volume of wood logged in this second-growth forest was between 210 and 220 cubic metres per hectare. If a conservative figure of 100 cubic metres per hectare is used as a benchmark for what is available in a first commercial thinning of second-growth forests across coastal BC, says Drushka, it amounts to a huge volume of wood, a volume that could save several thousand people from being laid off. "The other advantage you get out of that," he says, "is you've got lots of people employed in the woods in the European manner—increasing the value of the forests."

Furthermore, there's lots to suggest that some of the second-growth timber that is available right now is of good quality. With careful use, it can be used profitably by those who think carefully about how they mill it. For example, Primex Forest Products Ltd. processes second-growth and is one of a select few

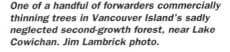

One of a handful of forwarders commercially thinning trees in Vancouver Island's sadly neglected second-growth forest, near Lake Cowichan. Jim Lambrick photo.

companies to have weathered the recent recession and posted healthy financial returns. These kinds of things are happening, albeit on a small scale, in many areas of BC. But the stories are told too rarely, lost amid the tonnes of ink and hours of air-time devoted to the endless conflicts over the logging of British Columbia's remaining old-growth.

Alternative logging

Mike Steeves is one man who has quietly worked in the shadows of valuable second-growth forests. Steeves is president of Texada Logging, a company with 17,000 acres of private forest, mostly on Vancouver and Saltspring islands. Steeves is also co-owner of SLT Shortlog Thinning, a company that has done selective logging for Pacific Forest Products and a bit for TimberWest (51 percent owned by Fletcher Challenge Canada Ltd.). "There are vast areas of second-growth that would benefit from thinning because they're overstocked," says Steeves. "If they're not, your growth rates decline, your stands stagnate and, I believe, they become more susceptible to disease, windthrow and snow damage."

Under Steeves' direction, loggers have done some clearcutting of these forests. But they've done a lot more alternative logging. They've done "conventional thinnings" of second-growth stands where smaller trees that are likely to die because of lack of light are logged, allowing the remaining trees to put on more volume. These thinnings and others have resulted in yields of between 70 and 150 cubic metres of wood per hectare logged. Rarely, Steeves says, is more than 30 percent of the volume removed from such stands, with half the logs being chipped for pulp and the remainder run through a sawmill: "We've also been doing group-selection cutting. It's where you have a very small clearcut. Generally the size of the clearcut should not exceed one-and-a-half times the tree height. And we've been using that system in older stands where there was a lot of root rot. We've been cutting the root rot pockets out and the area around the root rot pockets. And we've been pulling the stumps out of the ground, exposing the roots that have been affected to the air. And it works like a charm."

In 1988 Steeves invested in new automated European logging equipment that allowed trees up to 18 inches in diameter to be cut down and de-limbed. He also bought a light forwarder with low-pressure tires and a crane on the back capable of lifting the logs. The two machines allow a logging crew of five men to cut down about 36,000 cubic metres of wood a year, all of it in the form of thinning. They have proven so successful, Steeves says, that he recently purchased another two pair of machines.

There's room for a mixture of

New Forestry

The scientific background [of New Forestry] includes an increased understanding of:

• structure/function/composition relationships in old-growth forests, and the importance of specific structural features such as large trees, standing dead trees (snags), large downed logs, and the heterogeneous canopy structure;

• the extent to which such structures tend to persist through natural disturbance events such as wildfire or windstorms, providing "biological legacies" for the subsequent stand;

• the habitat value of early and late seral stages of forest management; and

• the importance of large-scale and long-term effects of forest management. Other research has focused on long-term site productivity and ecological resilience.

Doug Hopwood, "Principles and Practices of New Forestry: A Guide for British Columbians" (Ministry of Forests, Land Management Report Number 71, 1991).

logging activity in BC's coastal second-growth stands, some of which would be far more labour-intensive than the work Steeves' company does. But even if this kind of mechanized second-growth logging were expanded across Drushka's 500,000-hectare landscape, it yields a net increase of 416 jobs. And beyond the logging created in this thinning work there's the hauling and processing jobs. It's safe to say, based on today's sorry standard of one direct full-time job in BC's forest industry for every 1,000 cubic metres logged, that the current employment potential in BC's coastal second-growth forests is in the neighbourhood of 5,000 jobs. And that's just for wood provided from thinnings.

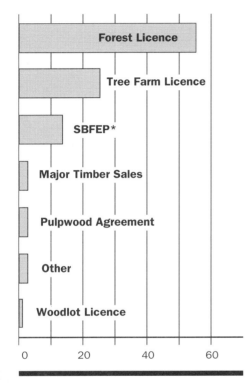

Second Helping

Forest tenure as a percentage of Annual Allowable Cut

* SBFEP signifies the Small Business Forest Enterprise Program

Source: Adapted from Richard Schwindt, Report of the Royal Commission of Inquiry into Compensation for the Taking of Resource Interests, Table 5–2 (1993).

The benefits of alternative logging are legion. It's better for the environment because it often utilizes lower-impact technologies whether they be horses or small skidders or cable yarders. It tends not to compromise biodiversity, tourism and recreation values as much, and it creates more jobs on the ground in logging and forest tending. It may, depending on the circumstances, require lower capital investments than conventional logging. And it doesn't demand huge volumes of wood in return to service the payments on that equipment. It can not only maintain the structure of old-growth ecosystems but, in its management approach to second-growth, it can even try to get some old-growth characteristics back. As Professor Haley notes: "Second-growth wood, on the sort of rotations we use, doesn't produce any clear wood. At 70–80, Douglas fir or hemlock or cedar produce no clear wood whatsoever unless you prune....But you can produce these clear grades by growing older trees....I think there is a strong argument that can be made for having some of the forests set aside on higher quality sites for longer rotations, maybe 150–200 years, periods over which we can extract a lot of non-timber benefits, we can practise selection logging because each tree is going to be extremely valuable and we can anticipate a product in the future which is a very high value. You can only do this economically if there is a high value per tree, yet we know that the high value is there."

It's time we seriously thought about ways to stretch out our old-growth supply, while trying to replicate its better qualities by allowing second-growth trees to stand longer before they're logged. "I can't think of an old-growth prime Douglas fir stand on east Vancouver Island," Steeves says. "I can't think of one. So why don't we set aside a second-growth stand now. We won't appreciate it, but our grandchildren will."

The structure of stewardship

Smith and Steeves are among only a handful of forest stewards nurturing the land in an environment where over 90 percent of the forest base is locked up by a few companies in long-term tenures. But in Scandinavia, where such a large cut is produced from a smaller land base of second-growth trees, both men would blend in with thousands of others who draw their livelihood from the forest. There are over 200,000 woodlot owners in Sweden, and almost 300,000 in Finland who regularly do the kind of work Smith and Steeves do. Here is a forest philosophy that places great importance on scale, that sees value in individuals working distinct, small parcels of land. Woodlots account for 64 percent of forest land ownership in Finland and half the forest land in Sweden. Each individual woodlot owner contributes only a small amount of wood in total, but together they represent a powerful force in Scandinavia's forest industry. To maximize economic returns for their efforts these women and men organize into associations to co-ordinate the processing and marketing of their timber. In BC, woodlot owners can only dream of doing so, hampered as they are by their weak numbers. There are fewer than 500 of them. And they log a pitifully small amount of wood, about 400,000 cubic metres or less than 1 percent of the allowable annual cut.

That this situation exists in BC is disconcerting as woodlots are widely acknowledged to be the best tenure for promoting forest stewardship, stable rural employment, and enhanced silviculture. Jack Bakewell, a retired forester who studied woodlot tenures in BC, says: "I don't think you can grow trees economically in this latitude with incremental silviculture using union and contract labour. A woodlot licensee with his family will donate a lot of time, and they see something down the line." This sort of thinking tends to be inimical to the commercial calculations of large companies. For one thing, there is simply

The culture of silviculture

Silviculture is not just a set of techniques, nor is it an occupation, a specialization or a profession. It involves more than the kind of knowledge which can be transmitted in institutions or by training. Neither is it something so subtle and refined as to be possessed only by a select and sensitive few. Silviculture is something a society acquires over time; it is the product of generations of experience. Silviculture advances as much from what is "wrong" as from what is "right". It embraces diversity and variety. It is a science as well as technology, and it is also an art which has as much to do with the psychology of the human beings who practice it as with the biological imperatives of a living, growing forest. It is not a luxury, an unaffordable dream, but a necessity....

The real solution lies not in intensive management or sustained yield, but in a profound change in our attitudes and relationship to the forest. Somehow we must learn to manage the forest in the same way that farmers manage their land. We must cease to be merely exploiters of the forest resource and become instead cultivators and nurturers....

In many respects, the situation is comparable to the effort of convincing a tribe of hunters and gatherers to invest their energies and resources in tilling the soil. Such transitions bring about what anthropologists call a "cultural shift," a period of conflict for the individuals directly involved and for their society. Given the primitive state of silviculture in North America, it is not surprising that cultural conflicts are developing as we shift from forest-cutting to a forest-farming economy, displacing as we do so many habits and hallowed concepts.

Ken Drushka, *Stumped: The Forest Industry in Transition* (Vancouver: Douglas & McIntyre, 1985).

---

not the return there. If, for example, a large forest company can get a 5 percent return investing its money in the bank, why put that money into a new forest that grows at a much slower rate? And if you are going to invest in new trees, why not do so in Alabama or Chile where the plantation growth rates are far faster? Similarly, this grunt work doesn't entice high-priced union labour where a much higher rate of return is necessary to make silviculture pay. Instead, silviculture is a separate industry that employs some 16,000 seasonal people province-wide. But it is an industry in the mold of the volume economy, composed of migrant firms low bidding for contracts from big forest companies. And their employees—often summer students from the city—fast-plant on a one-shot basis on remote mountainsides they will never see again.

The result is an industry with a dismal survival record, and an attitude to the forest that is far from the stewardship ethic exemplified by many woodlot owners. With hundreds of millions of government funds being poured into basic silviculture, planting levels have gone up in recent years. But that's about as far as it goes. Despite all the talk about the much-vaunted "crops" of second-growth, in 1992–93, only 196 hectares of Crown forest land were commercially thinned in the entire province, a tiny volume when compared with what is thinned in Finland and Sweden.

Like the family farm, silviculture is largely a job for sweat equity and landed stewards. "You can do thinning on a small scale," says Jack Bakewell, "but you've got to have small equipment. You've got to be thinking. It all comes down to economies of scale. If you've got great big machines that cost half a million bucks, they've got to operate in a big way. You're paying off a big investment in machinery and all the operating costs. A guy with small machinery or a horse, he's not moving much timber, but he's moving it and he's benefitting somewhere along the way. He's thinking that it's more of a personalized thing and he's got a

A troubling legacy. A neglected stand of sixty-year-old second-growth trees near Powell River. Commercially thinning this stand would improve tree growth and wood quality while providing much-needed new jobs.
Doug Radies photo.

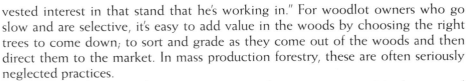
vested interest in that stand that he's working in." For woodlot owners who go slow and are selective, it's easy to add value in the woods by choosing the right trees to come down; to sort and grade as they come out of the woods and then direct them to the market. In mass production forestry, these are often seriously neglected practices.

With such potential, it is not surprising that numerous inquiries have urged that the number of woodlots be expanded. In 1988, a Ministry of Forests Report wanted the number doubled, but the recommendation was not followed. Five years later, the provincial Select Standing Committee on Forests, under the Chairship of Nelson–Creston MLA Corky Evans, issued a report entitled *Lumber Remanufacturing in British Columbia*. The report called for a five-fold increase in the allocation of the provincial cut to woodlots (bringing their level to 5 percent). It also called for the creation of a special log market involving woodlot owners, small sawmills and value-added manufacturers. As Evans commented on his hearings throughout the province: "The only people we met on our tour whose primary interest was growing trees were the woodlot operators."

But if woodlots are so efficient, the inevitable question arises: Why stop at 5 percent? A healthy diversity of alternative tenure arrangements from private woodlots to community forests and reduced corporate tenures holds the promise of better stewardship and higher productivity. But the changes are not coming. For one thing, a provincial bureaucracy used to dealing with a small number of big players doesn't relish the thought of working with a whole host of landowners and licensees. Nor do some unions, who see in a diversity of small players a much more difficult task in organizing their members. Finally, the major corporations are stiffly resistant to relinquishing control of their tenures. They've much to lose in an enhanced woodlot program that provides everything they don't—better management, higher valued timber, higher prices, more government revenues, and more wood on the market.

This kind of management is exemplified by people like Rod Gould, a horse logger and woodlot owner. On an early fall morning, on a stretch of forest well away from his home and woodlot in Greenwood, Gould is practising a kind of forestry like what he might do on his own parcel of land. At the side of a rough skid road travelling up a hill, Gould works some thick metal chains around two lodgepole pine logs. With the chains secured, he hauls himself onto a custom-built, two-wheel carriage about a metre off the ground. Grabbing the reins, he yells a command to his horses, and the pair, a fine cross of Belgian and Percheron, step forward pulling the slack out of the chains. There's a slight pause as the slack disappears and the horses strain to pull the logs from their resting places. Then they're off, clomping over the uneven ground, their breathing growing faster and louder as they near a pile of logs halfway down the hill.

It's 10:00 a.m., and Gould and his work partner will put in close to six hours more work before heading home. "I've been doing this for ten years. And that's all I've been doing. It's a viable way to make a living. But it's not an easy living. It's

Community forests in rural Japan

Forestry has evolved as a non-integrated industry, with the woodlands operations organized largely around cooperative village enterprises, and with a strong emphasis on afforestation, silviculture, and good resource management.

Private forest holdings in these towns are small, with between 65 and 71 percent of all holdings under 5 hectares. Community and temple forests are managed by community organizations and local forest owners, with residents providing free labour or the town contracting work by local loggers and silvilculturalists. Proceeds from community forests are used for local projects.

In their homes and public buildings, aesthetic sensitivities are nurtured, ancient rituals are practiced, and peace and harmony are prized. Wood, in the forms of polished centre poles, floor and wall panels, and furniture, is central to the aesthetic harmony. Such communities may seem stifling and static to young Japanese today, but however else one may characterize them, they do provide a conservationist and environmentally sensitive context for forests.

M. Patricia Marchak, "Global Markets in Forest Products: Sociological Impacts on Kyoto Prefecture and British Columbia Interior Forest Regions" (Paper prepared for *Journal of Business Administration*, special edition on forestry management policy, 1989).

satisfying but it's physically hard work," Gould says. He and his partner are selectively logging just under a third of the trees in this patch of forest. The Ministry of Forests won't allow any more trees to come down, for fear the forest canopy will open too much and the remaining trees become susceptible to

blowing down in a windstorm. Gould is working in, and will leave behind, a forest. That's a far cry from what's happening almost everywhere else around him. The trees in this forest are growing well, he says, and after this area is selectively logged the remaining trees will put on extra wood volume that other loggers will benefit from years or decades down the road.

On this day Gould and his part-ner will haul sixty trees out of the bush. In a week they'll cut down about three log truckloads worth of material. For their efforts they'll net about $200 a day in wages, as good as or even slightly better than a union logger's pay. "If I can't make $200 a day it isn't worth it," Gould says.

Horse logging is often dismissed by those in corporate and union boardrooms as an overly romanticized, somewhat dangerous form of labour, a throwback to a bygone era. But alternative logging is not just about horses—there are many technologies in use. And Gould, in turn, calls the industrial approach "ass backwards," an approach where efficiency means extracting or producing the maximum amount of material possible with the least amount of labour. This is an

approach that ignores, indeed des-troys, both social and environmental values, an approach where the true values of the woods are lost. And it is an approach that is increasingly unaccept-able to an international marketplace concerned about where wood comes from, and how it got to market.

For Gould, there are simply too many minuses and not a lot of pluses in allowing highly mechanized, conven-tional logging to run its course across the land base. That's why he prefers to take the definition of efficiency and turn it on its head, so that we might think more about employment and less about maximizing the volume of wood coming out of the bush. If this patch of

Horse logging in the Cariboo

Horse logging could potentially create a significant number of forestry jobs....It also creates new activity in the local agricultural economy. Since 6–10 cubic metres of wood, assuming highest quality selective logging, represents about one 12-hour day of work for a horse logger, a relatively small amount of wood can keep an individual working. A feller buncher, in contrast, moves about 400 cubic metres of wood per 12-hour day in normal operating conditions.

Horse logging is resurfacing

primarily because of the increasing role for low impact selective logging (e.g. near parks; in environmentally sensitive areas). The capital costs of horse logging are very low in comparison to conventional machine logging. The Cariboo is apparently a leader in horse logging in North America, and the number of workers has been increasing as acceptance grows in the industry and the Forest Service.

North Cariboo Community Futures, *Region in Transition: An Economic Profile and Development Strategy for the North Cariboo Region of BC* (1988).

Global market eyes sustainable wood

The need for working definitions of sustainable development is now expanding beyond international discussions on the environment into the trade area. Increasingly, some countries and consumers are indicating their preference for buying products only from "sustainably managed forests", and for assessing such products through codes and standards. While initially the focus of these efforts was on tropical timber, international attention is increasingly turning to include temperate and boreal forests (which account for slightly less than half of the world's forest resources).

There is an immediate need to develop an international consensus on a set of scientifically based criteria to distinguish sustainable from non-sustainable forestry practices. These criteria will serve two important goals: 1) to measure progress towards the goal of sustainable development; 2) to serve as the basis for identifying those products coming from sustainably managed forests.

"Criteria for the Sustainable Development of Canada's Forests," working paper prepared for the CSCE Seminar of Experts on the Sustainable Development of Temperate and Boreal Forests, Conference on Security and Co-operation in Europe (Montreal, September 27–October 1, 1993).

forest were clearcut with a feller buncher, about ten truckloads a day or 20 times as many trees as Gould logs would come down. If this patch of forest were clearcut, there might be one more job created. But there would be no more forest for children to admire, and no more trees left standing for another logger and his team of horses to work in decades down the road.

The promise of good wood

The promise of Smith and Steeves and Gould and many others today is the promise of wood from an industry based in a diversity of land stewards who

Cherryville children look at a recently logged hillside where alternative methods for cutting trees were successfully employed.
Jim Smith photo.

actually make the longer-term investments in the land that are so sorely lacking today. Many more individuals can be employed working our forests, especially if the government provides the incentives that will ensure long-term forest stewardship. These incentives may come in the form of reallocating existing second-growth and old-growth forest lands, over time, to smaller operators. Or, it may result in some individuals with proven track records gaining clear title to small parcels of forest, provided that BC develops a stringent forest practices code covering private lands. In other cases, communities themselves may be encouraged to take control of local forests, in order that the full range of interests will be represented in the management and use of those lands. Last but not least, corporate tenures will continue to play a significant role. But the scope of those holdings will necessarily be reduced, and the tenures redefined, to make way for alternatives and for drastically altered forest practices.

From logging contractors to environmental campaigners, from local economic development officers to lumber remanufacturers, even in the odd corporate boardroom itself, a growing number of people say we need more diversity in our timber holdings. With a multiplicity of smaller units, where people and communities play an active role in nurturing forests

A product that commands respect

Portland, Oregon-based Collins Pine recently became the first company in the United States to "certify" its wood....

Ensuring the sustainability of the forest has always been an important goal for Collins Pine, which has been owned by the Collins family for three generations....

One of the cornerstones of Collins Pine's management efforts is monitoring the status of 550 one-acre, old-growth plots that were established in the 1940s. These plots of sugar pine, ponderosa pine, white fir, Douglas fir, red fir and incense cedar hold a key to the dynamics of the forest; they tell foresters how quickly each tree is growing, whether the species composition has changed and

whether certain trees are dying. Changes in wildlife habitat are also noted.

From this information, the foresters glean the forest's growth in annual board feet per acre, and decide how much they can harvest in a year without overcutting....

The company also hand-picks the trees that should be harvested, focusing on removals that ensure the fastest growth of the remaining trees. Before harvesting, foresters check to see how rapidly a tree is growing, how well shaped it is, and how close it is to other trees. They ask: Is it a good source of seed for future crops? They remove the slow growing or the diseased trees that might affect those that remain.

Forest Perspectives, Portland OR (Vol. 3, Issue 3, Autumn 1993).

they consider their own, we can hope to develop a new approach that sees the land as something more than a fibre farm.

When asked what it would take to keep him fully employed in the woods, Bill McIntosh, a Vanderhoof woodlot owner, replied: about 1,200 hectares of forest, and the hiring of occasional labour. This is an infinitesimal amount of the total working forest base in BC—four ten-thousandths of 1 percent to be exact. And in more productive coastal or southern forests, the area needed would be lower still. Clearly, the potential to create thousands of new woodlot and community forestry jobs is enormous. And as more and more people return to the forest to draw a living from it, a new ethic will begin to emerge, a wood culture, because woodlot management inherently rewards value, not volume.

To listen to McIntosh and others who work their own land is to appreciate why the concept of value-added begins in the forest. If McIntosh doesn't treat his land well, he undermines his own well-being. That's why he tends to view his woodlot as a family estate, even if the estate is ultimately owned by the Crown. "What I am doing will be a benefit to my daughter," he says. "That's a lot different outlook than if I am an industrial forester working for a public company where it's tough to think that long-term." With a woodlot licence the only way to expand business is through silvicultural activities that grow better, more valuable trees. By spacing and pruning, woodlot owners realize big financial rewards when the trees they log are sold, particularly if the sales occur in competitive markets where the highest bidder gets access to the wood. Here is where the transition from a volume to a value economy must begin—in the woods.

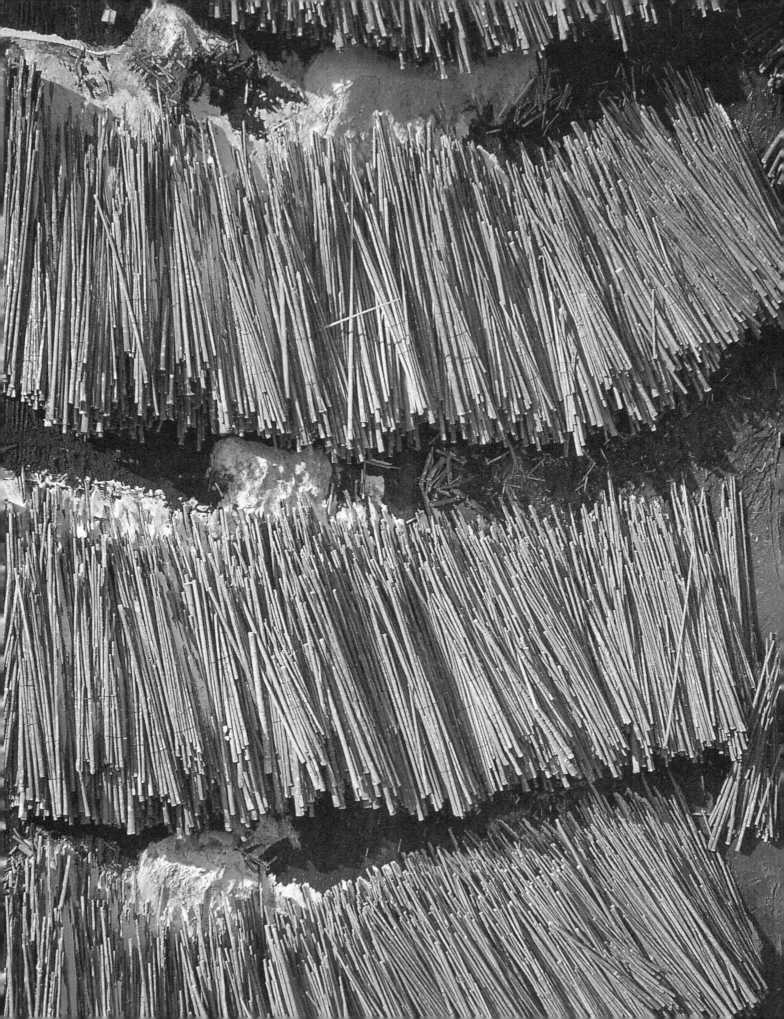

CHAPTER SEVEN

FINANCING THE TRANSITION

WHEN HERMAN HANS RECENTLY BID ON TIMBER through the Ministry of Forests' small business program he paid a big price—$106 a cubic metre to log 800 truckloads of wood. The sale was for a stand of trees on Kennedy Island, 48 km south of Prince Rupert. Situated at the western terminus of the Canadian National rail line, Prince Rupert is a major shipping point, well positioned to service the Pacific Rim. Despite this geographical advantage and the proximity of rich old-growth forests, the coastal community has never had much of a thriving wood processing industry. The Wedeene River mill, the last sizeable processor in the city, went into bankruptcy a number of years ago. The idled operation and its allocated Crown timber supply were subsequently bought by one of two major forest companies in the region, West Fraser Timber Co. Ltd.

Unlike Herman Hans and the region's other independent loggers, West Fraser doesn't bid for its logs. It doesn't need to as it has its own exclusive wood supply. Its timber comes from public lands where it is licensed to log trees under area-based Tree Farm Licences and volume-based Forest Licences. In return for its tenure holdings, West Fraser pays a fee for the timber, stumpage. It also pays for the roads and bridges it builds to get access to the wood, and for the costs of planting seedlings after clearcutting the old-growth forest. In West Fraser's case, it has also been told to re-open the Wedeene mill, something it promises to do in 1994.

Without that mill, indeed even with it, most trees logged on the north coast are processed elsewhere. For West Fraser, that means trucking logs east to Terrace, barging them south to the Lower Mainland and, until recently, shipping them overseas. The same applies to the biggest quota holder in the north coast, International Forest Products Ltd., which regularly barges wood to a host of timber-hungry sawmills in the Lower Mainland. People like Hans also sell a portion of their wood to offshore buyers, and the rest to the domestic market. But unlike West Fraser and Interfor, Hans pays more up front for the wood he logs, and he makes a lot less back.

Hans has operated his own logging business in the region since 1980, and what he's learned over the years troubles him. "Eighty-five percent of the timber

Craft industries, such as log home construction, extracts maximum dollar and employment value from BC's forests. Myron Kozak photo.

Opposite: Stacks of undervalued and underpriced logs in a mill yard near 100 Mile House. Al Harvey photo.

Tree of Knowledge

that's cut in the province does not see the market forces of supply and demand," Hans says. "The majors are not paying the true value of the timber they're cutting. And this has been going on for the last fifty years. So billions of dollars are being lost in uncollected stumpage." Despite our rapidly depleting old-growth, some trees held under licence by the majors in the north coast fell, until recently, to the chain saw at a cost of 25 cents a cubic metre. Those same companies often pay no more than $5 a cubic metre for the right to log old-growth. "On the cost side, they have roughly $8 to $10 more in costs," Hans says. "So if you add those extra costs it's $13 to $15 total stumpage, compared to me and most of the other small business loggers paying $40. So there's a difference of $25."

That spread allows companies like West Fraser to pay for acquisitions such as the purchase of the bankrupt Wedeene mill and its timber supply. It may also help West Fraser to pay for some of the costs of refurbishing the mill. To Hans and others who pay much more, West Fraser's low stumpage charges are a form of subsidy that has some pretty disquieting results. For instance, as the barges of old-growth logs head south, West Fraser and Interfor are permitted to claim the transport costs against their stumpage assessments, dramatically reducing what they pay to the province, and shortchanging Prince Rupert of its wood in the process. In the volume economy, the rationale for that subsidy is that it provides cheap wood to keep the big mills in Vancouver in the black. "Why should we allow that cost [allowance] for somebody who's got a building in the Lower Mainland?" asks Hans. "If they want the wood they should build a mill here." In the process, "the stumpage collected by the province would go up $7 to $9 a cubic metre."

Many small business loggers agree with Hans. If the market dictates what they pay, why shouldn't it be the same for the majors? Hans's solution is simple, but sweeping: "All Crown timber must go to log markets. There should be no appraisal system, no price set earlier. Anybody who's manufacturing should have no control over cutting rights. All timber really should be sold. And the processing facilities will buy logs on the open market. That's an ideal situation. Supply and demand would come into place." Like Hans, members of the Harcourt government realized that the stumpage prices paid by forest companies for Crown timber were too low. But its solution to the problem was to establish

new and higher stumpage rates by bureaucratic fiat rather than by market forces, which would generate even higher prices.

Small (business) is beautiful

The underdog status of Hans and his fellow market loggers isn't at all unusual. Quite the contrary. As a BC government study, *Strengthening Small Business in the 90s*, revealed, small businesses in BC across the board face a "pattern of truncated growth and premature failure." BC firms have the highest debt-to-equity ratio in Canada, a level of profits-to-sales that is 30 percent below the Canadian average, an overloaded reliance on debt financing, and, for firms outside the Lower Mainland, a serious lack of access to startup financing.

These are also the very firms on which BC's economic success increasingly depends. During the booms and busts of the 1980s, for example, while the number of medium and large firms declined, small businesses with fewer than 20 employees increased by over 30,000. One of those businesses was Hans's company, Biport Forest Products, which has about 15 full-time employees, not including office staff and sub-contractors, who are paid an average annual wage of $40,000. Between 1979 and 1987 small businesses created fully 85 percent of the net new jobs in the province. Another recent government study, *Small Business In British Columbia*, concluded: "Small businesses proved to be more adaptable than larger businesses, and better able to respond to changing economic conditions and fluctuating markets."

Whether it's woodlot owners or furniture makers, small businesses are the underpinning of the emerging new value economy. Established big-volume firms like West Fraser still dominate the economy, however, employing more people and generating more economic activity overall in BC. This dominance is maintained with a raft of direct and indirect subsidies, the most obvious of which are the low resource rents or stumpage payments. But the subsidies don't stop there. For example, every year BC loses over $80 million in forest productivity from the soil degradation associated with poor logging practices. Similarly, since the late 1980s, well over $500 million in taxpayers' money has gone to replant clearcuts, a sort of retroactive subsidy. Is it any wonder with this kind of money being sucked up to pay for the earlier actions of our forest industry that new businesses with new ideas have so much trouble accessing capital? Numerous government programs to help small businesses do exist, of course, programs with laudable labels like the small business venture capital program, the employee investment program, and the regional seed capital program. But the government's first commitment is to prop up the existing volume economy and, just as most tenures go to the big companies, so do the program dollars. For example, the Industrial Development Branch of the Ministry of Economic Development, Small Business and Trade provided assistance to major companies such as Louisiana Pacific, Slocan Forest Products, Celgar Pulp, Orenda Pulp and Paper, Ainsworth Lumber and Vanderhoof Pulp and Paper. Louisiana Pacific received $5 million in 1991–92 for infrastructure costs for a new pulp mill in Chetwynd. That same year the Economic Development Ministry provided the Council of Forest Industries with $2.2 million for its operations. In comparison, small business programs are starved of the resources they need to make a real dent in the industry.

Clearly, making a transition to Forestopia will cost money. Developing programs and proper financing mechanisms for new businesses requires funding, the deficit notwithstanding. To make that transition depends less, however, on finding more money than on changing the manner in which existing capital resources are allocated, and by using those resources more efficiently. Politicians may be vocally supportive of small businesses, but they are loath to bite the financial bullet and redirect resources away from the inefficient, but large and

Small Businesses / Big Appetites
Share of job creation by firm size

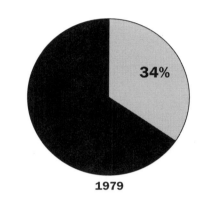

1979

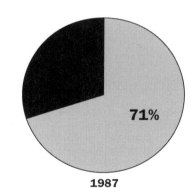

1987

☐ Businesses with less than 20 employees

■ Businesses with more than 20 employees

Source: Ministry of Regional and Economic Development, Small Business in British Columbia 1979–1989: A Decade of Change *(1990).*

powerful, players in the volume economy. As the Forest Renewal Act recognizes, this is the place to start in financing the transition. We need to get control of the capital we have in order to ensure that it's used more efficiently.

There's magic—and money—in the market

Since the 1940s, BC's forest policy has reflected the simple premise that a company's right to cut timber was matched by a parallel obligation to mill it. The thinking behind this policy was that when manufacturing facilities had a secure supply of timber through long-term forest tenures, investors would find BC attractive, new infrastructure would be built, and all of this would enhance the value of the public's timber resource. In hindsight, however, only some of it proved correct. Forest industry capital has indeed come to BC and a wealthy provincial economy been created. But only in the last decade have timber values and resource rents begun to rise, and then largely as a result of external pressure from US timber interests.

Today, criticisms of this system of privileged access to the forest are legion, extending well beyond the special interests of US competitors, and focussing on the lack of true, effective markets in determining timber value. From a resource viewpoint, the lack of markets results in economic and environmental waste. With buyers being unable to bid on and set a true price for tenured wood, high-value timbers are simply lumped in with those

Some of the highest prices paid for wood anywhere are fetched at this unique log sorting and selling yard in Lumby. That's because each company buying wood competes against a host of other bidders. Most everywhere else in the province, companies are sheltered from market forces.
Jim Smith photo.

of low value, and the incentive to add value is undermined. So long as the costs of cutting timber are kept low, cheap commodity products return profits, even though the wood is actually worth much more. This is the nature of the "value-subtracted" critique proposed by Mike Major: prized old-growth towering high above the forest floor ends up not as tongue-and-groove flooring but as rough-cut lumber sold to disappear behind the gyproc wall.

This way of allocating our resources began in the late 1940s when virgin forests still blanketed much of the province, and timber supplies were still plentiful. The pattern was set, and as the forest economy expanded, it remained stuck in that pattern. A simple, if somewhat gluttonous, economic formula came to dominate our thinking and our practices: Profits = low wood costs + high wood volumes. Just as in the 1950s, today's forest economy still requires cheap raw materials to produce the low-value commodity two-by-fours on which its established markets depend. Breaking this pattern is the single most important contribution we can make to financing an economic transition to a new forest economy.

Recall for a minute the "alternative logging" described in Chapter 6. Imagine those logs going to local log yards where they are sorted by species and grade. Then imagine the logs selling under bid at an average price almost four times higher than average stumpage rates. You'd then be close to envisioning a remarkable program already underway in Lumby, near Vernon. The Lumby market, and a similar project on Vancouver Island involving the Duncan and Port Alberni forest districts, are the work of the Ministry of Forests' small business program. They are the end component in a scheme designed to test whether alternative logging systems can be profitable. And the early evidence says they can be indeed. The Lumby project, overseen by Jim Smith, has shown that alternative logging that employs more people can be married with a market that creates jobs and provides a healthy return to the government.

"Yesterday we got an average of $105 a cubic metre," Smith said in November 1993, the day after another successful log sale at the Lumby sorting yard. "Obviously we're going to make money, we're going to make lots of money, by selling our logs through a log yard. And I think we've proven beyond a shadow of a doubt that you can do these alternate silvicultural [logging] systems and make money." Smith is quick to caution that the costs associated with running the logging program and the Lumby log yard are high. But they are more than recovered, because the market is allowed to work. In total, it cost about $28.50 a cubic metre to log; another $4.94 a cubic metre to run the log yard, which employed seven people full-time; 90 cents a cubic metre to rent the log yard; and $3 each for road building and tree planting. Finally, the administration of the unique program cost the Ministry of Forests between $4 and $5 a cubic metre. The total cost was $45 a cubic metre. But the average bid price for the timber was more than double that. So, after all the costs associated with the program were subtracted, companies paid an average stumpage of more than $45 a cubic metre compared to the average appraised stumpage rate in the Vernon area of about $11 a cubic metre. Even with the promised increases under the Forest Renewal Plan, average stumpage prices in the Vernon area would only rise to $17.60 a cubic metre, or 39 percent the rate at the Lumby yard.

The key to the Lumby log market's success lies in sorting the logs by species and grade before bids are called. In this way, the highest prices are ensured for what is sold all down the line from the prime, clear spruce logs to the knot- and defect-riddled pine. While the market is still in its infancy, and there is doubt about whether more wood will be allocated to it given current tenure arrangements, the prices paid clearly show there is huge money to be made in a competitive setting. People will pay top dollar for top quality wood. And when they pay more up front for what they get, they'll do more with it back at the mill.

In early January 1994, Len Thiessen, a Cherryville mill owner, inspected some high-quality over-sized spruce logs at the Lumby yard and offered to pay a record $200 a cubic metre for the wood. It would cost, on average, $1,000 for each log Thiessen purchased. But he was prepared to pay because the end product he made would fetch at least twice that price. Each log would be run through Thiessen's circular saw and cut into defect-free pieces measuring 5 mm thick by 9 inches wide and 24 inches long. "This wood has to be clear. You cannot do anything with this wood with knots. It must be straight-grained, with 12 to 24 growth rings per inch," Thiessen explains. These rigid specifications must be met because the wood will later be carefully re-cut into guitar tops by an instrument-maker. "You don't just go out into the forest and cut down any oversized spruce and use it," Thiessen says. "This is why the price is so high, why you can pay so much. It's a very specialized product. It's value-added."

The happy story of the Lumby yard and the innovative value-added wood manufacturing it spawns, however, is the exception to the rule. By keeping timber

Who cares for the forest?

In economic terms, what results from the forest tenure arrangements in British Columbia is a system in which no one, whether in private industry or in the public sector, has the incentive or ability to invest in the resource itself....Tenure holders have spent their investable funds on building, expanding or modernizing their plant facilities, or on acquiring other companies in the industry. If they have declined to invest these funds on a voluntary basis in the resource, it is because they have not been obliged to, or the system has not encouraged them to do so. The public sector has undertaken intermittent efforts at financing forest renewal and improvement....In all these cases, however, these programs failed to survive beyond the next election, a time when budgets tend to be directed to other priorities.

Truck Loggers' Association, "BC's Forests: A Vision for Tomorrow" (Working papers, 1990).

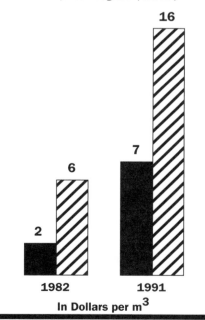

Bidding Up The Price
Stumpage paid by the Majors (TFL/FL) compared with the Small Business Forest Enterprise Program (SBFEP)

In Dollars per m³

■ TFL/FL Stumpage Rate
▨ SBFEP Stumpage Rate

Source: Adapted from G. J. McDade, "Report on Compensation Issues Concerning Protected Areas: A Draft Discussion Paper", Table 4-3 (Vancouver: Sierra Legal Defence Fund, 1993); stumpage from Ministry of Forests Annual Report 1991–92.

A restorative economy

Without doubt the single most damaging aspect of the present economic system is that the expense of destroying the earth is largely absent from the prices set in the marketplace. A vital and key piece of information is therefore missing in all levels of the economy. This omission extends the dominance of industrialism beyond its useful life and prevents a restorative economy from emerging.

Paul Hawken, *The Ecology of Commerce* (HarperBusiness Publications, 1993).

values low, the provincial government has let huge sums of money slip through its hands and, in the process, suppressed the incentives which would emerge with a market system. At the logging end of the process low returns discourage the forest stewardship on which sustainability depends. At the other end of the process, in the mill, low wood costs discourage the value-added innovation which comes when raw materials are valued highly. Were logs selling at market prices, companies would be forced to add value out of sheer financial necessity. Thus does the market work its invisible hand, encouraging those who participate in it to sort and grade, to conserve and allocate efficiently, in short, to find value where none existed before. In return, the higher monies flowing back can be reinvested in enterprises that improve the value of the trees we'll log in future generations, or help finance new local businesses.

In addition to massive revenue losses, BC's non-market forest economy has skewed the whole geography of the province's economic development. We have, Mike Major told a committee of the provincial legislature, "a hinterland economy in BC" where the costs of logging are imposed in one area, and the benefits accrue somewhere else. This is because profits are made where the processing, not the cutting, takes place: "We've allowed the values to be extracted in the urban areas. We don't assign a very high value to logs in British Columbia, and what moves from the rural areas are logs….The rural areas, wherefrom the timber originates, are essentially exploited in a sense that is not distinctly different from the kind of colonial exploitation that we've known in the past, especially in Third World countries."

Resisting the magic

Shifting from a non-market to a market-responsive economy is not easy. One need only look at experiences in Russia and Eastern Europe to see that. While BC is not like Russia or the Third World, one similarity is striking. Be they authoritarian political parties, intransigent state officials, unaccountable multinational corporations or big union bureaucracies, everywhere the beneficiaries of the non-market status quo are big and powerful institutions that resist dynamic change from below. Certainly the prime beneficiaries of BC's tenure system have been the large integrated companies. Through acquisitions and mergers, tenure has become consolidated in fewer and fewer hands. Meanwhile, cut levels have shot skyward and now dramatically exceed those agreed to under the original tenures.

Ironically, tenures were supposed to ensure social stability through the so-called "appurtenance" clause in some tenure contracts that required milling facilities to be maintained as a condition of tenure. Instead, the agreement is often ignored allowing mills like Gitwangak to be closed down with the loss of many jobs. Meanwhile, attempts to introduce market mechanisms into this tenured system are regularly resisted and thwarted. In the coast region that stretches from Vancouver to Prince Rupert, for example, the so-called Vancouver Log Market provides the one functioning market in the industry. The region represents a little over 30 percent of the provincial cut. But perhaps the most significant character of the Vancouver Log Market is the controversy it has generated as a true price setter. That's because 87 percent of the coastal timber supply is controlled by just ten firms, and fully 70 percent by just five. Moreover, these firms often trade, rather than buy and sell logs. Throughout it all, the Council of Forest Industries maintains a close, if informal, monitoring role. As one consultant's report concluded: "Its transactions consist primarily of trades between the seven major tenure holders who hold 90 percent of the AAC in tree farm licences and forest licences in the Vancouver Forest Region. These firms are all represented on the COFI log market group, joined by leading log brokers, and by a few of the handful of remaining `independents' in the wood products group on the Coast."

This situation has led people like University of BC professor Peter Pearse to dismiss the prices that the market generates because of the predominance of a few large traders engaged in swap transactions. One just cannot be confident that the prices reflect the full value of the logs, Pearse says. In 1990, a special committee of the BC legislature chaired by Social Credit MLA Graham Bruce agreed, finding that the Vancouver Log Market exhibited "features inconsistent with a freely competitively driven marketplace" and recommending instead the establishment of a British Columbia Log Market. That report died a quiet death.

One government initiative that did succeed was the expansion in 1988 of the Small Business Forest Enterprise Program (SBFEP). By extracting 5 percent of the timber held under other forms of tenure, the government allocated over 9 million cubic metres either to straight competitive sales where the highest bidder won the logging rights, or to special "bid proposal" sales where the main criterion was the value to be added to the timber sold. People like Herman Hans get access to some of this wood, and pay a high price for it. But to COFI and its member companies the takeback amounted to breaking a contract. When it was announced, dire warnings issued forth from the corporate towers of Burrard and Georgia streets that investor confidence in BC's forest industry was eroding, that forest companies here were considering investing in so-called safer business climates. But for small logging outfits and remanufacturers alike, the attitude was, and is, exactly the opposite. To them, the program is seen as the only mechanism currently available to ensure that the majors don't take it all.

One such remanufacturer is Gian Sandhu. Sandhu runs Jackpine Forest Products in Williams Lake, a remanufacturing mill that's secured a steady supply of lumber to re-cut in its mill from one of the major sawmills in town, Lignum Ltd. With timber awarded under the small business program, Sandhu has the necessary leverage to cement trade deals. With the awarding of the timber, Sandhu was also able to invest $2.8 million in his plant and start re-cutting lumber into an array of high-value components. Sandhu is blunt in his assessment of what would happen to companies like his without the small business program. The value-added industry, he says, "would die. In the Interior, I can guarantee you, it would die." And the reason is simple. Given the lack of a true market, remanufacturers like Sandhu have no clout in a system that grants monopoly control to a select few.

Despite its success, the small business program, particularly the competitive timber sales, has stirred up accusations that the big forest companies are meddling and manipulating. The most serious accusation is that of so-called

Dead in the water: without guaranteed supplies of wood, successful remanufacturers like Gian Sandhu of Williams Lake-based Jackpine Forest Products would not be in business.

surrogate bidding where small companies bid for wood at the behest of the majors. Subsidized by cheap wood from their tenures, the large licensees can afford to cover their incremental wood needs with the more expensive market wood and, in doing so, out-price smaller operators. One independent sawmiller, Charles Merriam from Cherryville, was so incensed at the practice in his area that he complained to the Canadian Federation of Independent Business that "over 90 percent of the wood allocated to the SBFEP ends up in the hands of the large

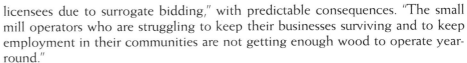

licensees due to surrogate bidding," with predictable consequences. "The small mill operators who are struggling to keep their businesses surviving and to keep employment in their communities are not getting enough wood to operate year-round."

What this suggests is that partial attempts to open up the market leave the system open to manipulation by the major companies. Obviously, if the market is to work effectively, the province must free up greater portions of timber for sale, and it must separate, in part or whole, production facilities from timber management. To level the playing field, says Hans, "we must level the tenure system."

No market without perestroika

Rejecting the old premise of appurtenance by instituting a market gulf between loggers and processors has long been a popular idea. Numerous committees and commissions have come to this conclusion—the 1974 Task Force on Timber Disposal, the 1976 Royal Commission on Timber Rights and Forest Policy, the 1990 Select Standing Committee on Forests and Lands and the 1991 Forest Resources Commission (FRC). As the FRC concluded in its first public report: "In essence, the Commission sees a tenure system that significantly reduces the volume of timber now controlled by a relatively small number of large corporations, and transfers that freed-up volume to the development of a competitive log market . . . The Commission believes that the establishment of a province-wide log market represents the only way that the province can realize full value for its resources."

Why then has the idea foundered? Because one can't have a dynamic market without a diversity of buyers and sellers, exactly what's missing in BC. On the selling side, this means an extensive network of managers in the forests such as underpins the system in Scandinavia. In other words, we need tenure reform, and the optimum candidates for new forest tenures—specialized stewardship companies, woodlot owners, Native bands, local communities—are very different from what we have today. With such short investment horizons, today's large corporate tenure-holders clearly aren't the best candidates to manage forests that require centuries rather than decades of nurturing. But they will continue steadfastly to oppose reform because it takes away the one thing that makes their tenure holdings valuable—cheap timber. This proposed change undoubtedly unsettles Ministry of Forests officials as well. After all, a vastly expanded market would upset the present system of administered prices, and semi-private or community-owned forest lands would fundamentally alter the nature of Crown control of BC's timber lands. This may go some way to explaining why both the Social Credit government that appointed the FRC and the NDP government that followed it failed to act on the tenure changes the commission proposed.

On the buying side, markets will only function well if diverse end users compete on equal terms. Today, this is the biggest obstacle facing remanufacturers in their struggle against the well-financed majors. Without protection and assistance for the smaller players, major companies can easily lock up supplies on an open market, achieving through private contracts with forest owners what they lost through tenure reform.

Bill Markvoort, a registered professional forester and president of the Independent Timber Marketing Association, would like to see half of all Crown timber sold competitively. The bid prices would then dictate what stumpage rates companies were charged on their tenured holdings. Once these market and tenured prices were in equilibrium, Markvoort believes it would no longer be possible for the major companies to corner the market. "It would reduce the inherent advantage that tenure holders have in the timber and log marketplace,

Poor credit, no wood

Credit is a major impediment to supply for many remanufacturing plants. I have been on both sides of the fence when it comes to selling and buying lumber. There is no doubt that most remanufacturing plants are not only underfinanced and may be a poor credit risk with most suppliers, but they are also perceived, regardless of their size or age, to be a credit risk. I cannot stress this point too strongly. Many times wood is "not available" or "sold out" strictly because the lumber salesman doesn't need, or doesn't want, the hassle of slow collections. The wood is generally available if you have the ability to pay for it and have the confidence of the lumber salesman to pay for it each and every time.

David Verchere, President, Vewest Products, Vancouver, quoted in *Report of Proceedings of the Select Standing Committee on Forests, Energy, Mines and Petroleum Resources* (Issue 15, Williams Lake, January 25, 1993).

putting all market participants on an equal footing," he said, and such a system would have the added benefit of ensuring that BC would no longer be "subject to a countervail [duty on softwood lumber] based on lack of competition."

Large revenues are at stake here, revenues that could well finance the transition to Forestopia. As Jim Smith's experience in Lumby attests, with careful work and expeditious sales, huge sums of money are to be made through log markets. In the Kamloops Forest Region, which takes in Lumby and area, the average stumpage paid in 1991–92 was a little more than $7 a cubic metre, $38 below the stumpage paid in Lumby after all costs were deducted. On the 68.5 million cubic metres of timber cut on Crown lands that year, this difference would have increased government revenues by $2 billion. This is more than the province's entire annual deficit, leading one to wonder whose budget is supporting whom!

This is admittedly a very rough calculation. But the scale of the figure is not out of line. For example, in 1992 the American Department of Commerce calculated that the costs to British Columbia of denying log markets both domestically and internationally were nearly 17 percent of the costs of product shipments, or almost $1.5 billion a year. Moreover, with timber costs in other jurisdictions running well above British Columbia's, to talk of doubling or even tripling the public revenues from our forests is not wildly optimistic. In BC, recent experience points in exactly this direction. The kind of bid prices fetched in Lumby are in keeping with log market trials on Vancouver Island where logs recently sold for $118 a cubic metre. The only difference is that the wood sold on Vancouver Island was culled not from ancient old-growth forests but from newer second-growth stands! Companies like Primex not only mill those logs at a profit but post some of the best financial returns in the industry in doing so. And Primex is one of a few large companies on the coast to have little timber secured under tenure, holding cutting rights to only about 7 percent of its milling needs. If Primex can do it with excellent returns on assets, there's no reason others can't.

Stemming the invisible flows

Opening and expanding log markets is an important element in financing the transition to the new forest economy. But other financing tools are also available, particularly at the community level. In the northwest corner of the province, in communities like Prince Rupert and Stewart, a central fact of life is the shipment of raw materials to large overseas markets or big urban centres such as the Lower Mainland. Accompanying this highly visible flow of raw logs is an all-but-invisible exodus of investment capital.

In Prince Rupert, the province's twentieth-largest credit union operates with an asset base of $150 million, about 20 percent of which is available for investment. Portions of this large pool of money could, in the right environment, be channelled into loans for local business development in a variety of sectors, including forestry. But that's not happening, says Mike Tarr, president and chief executive officer of Kaien Consumers Credit Union. "Clearly our mission, or our purpose in life, should be in focussing on the local community and region," Tarr says. "And to the extent that we can do that, we do. But more and more we're forced to look elsewhere. We simply don't have enough investment opportunities."

"Up here we're dependent first on the fishing industry and then on a local pulp mill," Tarr continues, adding both industries are in trouble. "When I'm doing my strategic planning for this credit union, I have to be honest, we do a significant amount of our business in the Lower Mainland, and have for the last several years, because there's just not enough growth in our region."

Tarr, who is also chairman of the BC Central Credit Union, would like to

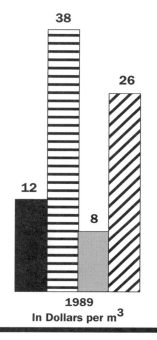

Sold Short
Comparison of US Pacific Northwest and BC Net Stumpage Rates for 1989

1989
In Dollars per m^3

■ BC Coast Stumpage Rate
PNW Coast Stumpage Rate
BC Interior Stumpage Rate
PNW Interior Stumpage Rate

Source: G. J. McDade, "Report on Compensation Issues Concerning Protected Areas: A Draft Discussion Paper", Table 4-1 (Vancouver: Sierra Legal Defence Fund, 1993).

see depositor funds channelled into the local economy rather than things like the Lower Mainland's booming real estate market. But until the provincial government takes the problems seriously enough that it helps local communities develop their own economic strategies, it's impossible for him to do otherwise.

Tarr says one way to harness credit union investment in local business development is for forestry-dependent communities to gain control of the management and sale of their natural resources. Again, when stumpage revenues accrue to the province, they flow out of the local area into the general revenue fund in Victoria, just as surely as the logs and investment dollars flow down to Vancouver. If, on the other hand, Prince Rupert operated its own log market and channelled the revenues from its log sales back into a local forestry development fund, the credit union could then extend loans to local companies that wanted to manufacture that wood. All the community would have to offer the credit union in return, Tarr says, is "some form of guarantee" that the loan, or a portion of it, would be covered.

Of course, such a scenario would mark a major change in how our Crown resources are allocated and administered. But given the current state of affairs in which the provincial government loses money running the Ministry of Forests, this is not a bad thing. In 1991–92, for example, the provincial government collected $608 million in stumpage and other payments from forest companies but its expenditures were $667 million. Two hundred thousand hectares of forest were logged and the Ministry of Forests failed to turn a profit. This is not where the provincial government collects the bulk of its money from the industry: the biggest chunk of money—more than $1 billion annually—comes from taxes on workers' wages and, corporate taxes. But the downstream revenue source is there regardless; its existence is no excuse for the money lost in administering the stumpage system.

One community where the local credit union is starting to play a new and exciting role in economic development is Nanaimo. The Nanaimo Credit Union has an asset base of $252 million and a membership in excess of 20,000. Don McMillan, general manager of the Central Island Community Development Society (CICDS), recently achieved his longtime goal: a working partnership with the credit union. Through the federal government's very successful Community Futures Program and the private sector, CICDS accesses about $1 million annually to carry out a variety of projects. It's not a lot of money in the scheme of things, but it's enough to help individuals and small groups of people get started in their own businesses. A typical client is a welder who's been laid off from a job at a local mill. He wants to strike out on his own, but he lacks the knowledge or the finances to establish his own business. Through CICDS he can get the technical expertise and often the startup capital to get going. In this way, CICDS has helped more than 300 businesses start in the last four years, 70 percent of which are still operating, a great success rate considering eight out of ten small businesses fail within the first five years of operation.

If there is a problem with the program it is that it has become too popular, placing a strain on the financing end of the operation. And that's what got McMillan to thinking about the local credit union. Under the new agreement, the credit union has agreed to take over CICDS's bankable loans. McMillan says the new deal is a winner for all concerned. Under CICDS's loan terms, a borrower pays 10 percent interest or prime plus 3. Through the credit union he probably pays prime plus 1 or prime plus 2, a significant savings. "It's a win-win situation," says McMillan. For the client it establishes a relationship with a conventional lender at a lower interest rate. For the credit union it provides a new account, which in turn broadens the economic base for its members. CICDS wins because it now has capital freed up to help other aspiring business people.

And finally, and perhaps most importantly, it keeps capital, goods and services circulating within the community rather than flowing out.

And this is just for starters

Reforms of log markets and local control of revenues are only two of the financing tools available to a government with a vision and a commitment to transition. Credit union assets in BC total some $14 billion, and credit unions are by their nature committed to local communities. Yet they are financial institutions, so they are wary of backing new ventures without some form of collateral or government support.

As well as credit unions, government-backed development banks exist in several jurisdictions, and could be profitably applied to rural BC. Ontario has recently pioneered an innovative program establishing "community loan funds" and "community investment share corporations" throughout the province, with 100 percent backing from the provincial government for the principal invested by residents. Venture capital funds, including ethical investment funds, could be encouraged and dramatically expanded in community-based investment, as could the use of pension fund monies.

The list of financing techniques is as long and tested in other jurisdictions as it is neglected in this one. One thing is clear, though: money itself is not the problem. The funds are there; solutions abound. But, like perestroika abroad, the transition to a value economy will not succeed with half measures.

BC Inc.

Guaranteed action

If the credit union did not have to assume some of the risk associated with placing funds locally and could [do so] by virtue of a government guarantee program...then the credit union has a capacity to try and move things more positively within their own local community...and there are programs out there—small business development programs and so on—that the federal and provincial governments have been involved in for some time, where a guarantee system has been implemented and works.

Ross Gentleman, Ministry of Finance Financial Institutions Commission (FICOM), and co-founder of CCEC (Community Congress for Economic Change) Credit Union. Personal communication (July 1993).

Successful development banks south of the border

With appropriate federal involvement, community development lending can help reduce poverty, counter social and political disenfranchisement, and stoke the engines of economic growth. Community Development Finance Institutions combine an understanding of the people and communities they serve with the business expertise needed to operate a strong financial institution. As a result, they successfully lend to borrowers that conventional institutions shun. The four community development banks (Shorebank Corporation in Chicago, Community Capital Bank in Brooklyn,

Southern Development Bancorporation in Arkansas, and the Center for Community Self-Help in North Carolina) have collectively made more than $400 million in community development loans with loan loss rates at or below the level of their peer depository institutions.

Coalition of Community Development Finance Institutions, *CDFIs: Key Tools for Rebuilding Communities* (Yardley PA, January 1993).

Innovations in Ontario

The Community Investment Share Corporation (CISC) and the Community Loan Fund (CLF) programs were developed in response to the recognition that the renewal and growth of local economies is often hampered by a lack of access to capital...the CLF and CISC programs address these gaps in credit and equity markets by enabling communities to establish new types of investment vehicles. Communities can use these vehicles to direct investment to local enterprises thereby expanding their local capacity to create jobs....

Investors will be protected by a 100% guarantee on invested principal...returns are modest and/or investors are obligated to be very patient with their capital. In return, they receive assurance that their principal is safe and that the funds will be put to active use in building the economic resilience of their community.

Ontario Ministry of Municipal Affairs, "Community Economic Development Financing Mechanisms" (Discussion paper, June 1993).

Local money for local projects

In 1985, the Quebec Federation of Labour launched Fonds de Solidarité des Travailleurs with a $10 million loan from the federal government. Individuals who invest in the fund receive a 20% tax credit from both the federal and provincial government and the investment qualifies for RRSP purposes. Solidarité is now the largest venture capital fund in Canada, with more than $380 million under management, and a mandate to invest in fledgling Quebec-based businesses.

Jacques Sayegh, "Venture Capital Redefined," in *Canadian Banker* (Vol. 99, No. 3, May–June 1992).

The power of pension funds

Community Development organizations suggest that the largest impediment to economic development [is] the gap in capital markets for certain groups of economic players. Capital gaps represent investment opportunities. State governments reap a double return when pension funds target these opportunities. First, the pension funds win by diversifying their investment portfolios and earning an acceptable return. Second, communities win when fund investors provide capital for housing, jobs, and other capital needs.

Center for Policy Alternatives, "Background Paper on Economically Targeted Investments" (Washington DC, 1993).

CHAPTER EIGHT

CREATING VALUE

FOR THE FRESHMAN MLA FROM NELSON–CRESTON, IT WAS A crowning moment. A small business logger first elected to the Legislature in 1991, Corky Evans rose in the chamber to submit his report as chairperson of the Select Standing Committee on Forests. Evans was pleased and excited with what his committee had done.

"Basically this is the deal, Honourable Speaker," he began, and then he told of his plan to open up the lumber manufacturing sector to the little guys who could "add value" and make a difference. "Wherever we went," Evans said, "people in the forest-dependent communities realized that the industry is in transition....There are issues out there that are nonpartisan in nature, the answers to which benefit all British Columbians, regardless of what party affiliation or philosophy we might bring to addressing the problems."

Nonpartisan perhaps, but not uncontroversial. Months earlier, in Williams Lake, Evans and other MLAs representing British Columbia's three major political parties had heard a very different story from the head of an association representing the region's biggest logging companies and lumber mills. "We believe that the view that value-added is the panacea—the only way to get more from our timber resource—has been overstated," said Van Scoffield, general manager of the Cariboo Lumber Manufacturers' Association. "In reality, the production of commodity products will continue to be the mainstay of BC's forest industry for some time to come. I would say that it's likely to remain that way as far down the road as we can see."

To Scoffield, the major tenure holders have good ideas of their own, and can create more value-added products—door jambs, mouldings, stairway components, window stock—themselves. Moreover, they maintain that redirecting a portion of their allocated timber supply for smaller companies is unwise and akin to breaking past contracts. But Scoffield went even further, calling value-added mills inherently unstable, not the sort of ventures to build a vibrant economy on. His attitude is common in an industry that maintains that what's good for the company is good for the company town, and good for British Columbia.

But the all-party committee wasn't biting at the bait. Among those to question Scoffield was Kenneth Jones, Liberal MLA for Surrey–Cloverdale. "In previous representations we heard the suggestion that perhaps 50 percent of the wood supply should be allocated to an open market to allow the remanners to get better access to it. How would you, as representative of your manufacturers, deal with such a proposal?"

Scoffield's answer was unequivocal: "In a nutshell, I would say our fear is not only the morality of such a radical change and about backtracking on contractual commitments, but also that the substitution of, say, 50 percent—taking half the quota away from a sector that is essentially quite stable and giving it to a sector

The deal

Basically this is the deal, Hon. Speaker. It's an incredibly complicated subject, and I tried to reduce it to an image that we can all grasp. The trees in BC belong to the people. People sell, say, a logging truckload of wood—everybody knows what they look like—that carries 35 cubic metres of wood. That truckload can be cut into commodity lumber we are all used to—2-by-6s, 2-by-8s, or 2-by-12s— and in the process it will create 30 person-hours of work. Or you could take the same truckload of wood and turn it into furniture, doors, windows or desks and create 160 person-hours of work. It seems to me that the mark of our intelligence as leaders and political will as elected representatives in BC, in the management of timber at least, is how close we can get to that second number, with as many truckloads as possible.

Corky Evans, MLA for Nelson-Creston, speaking in the BC Legislative Assembly (in *Hansard*, Vol. 10, No. 19, June 3, 1993).

Opposite: Karl Lange puts the finishing touches on a Douglas fir raised panel door at British Columbia Door Company Ltd. The Vancouver-based company makes between 12,000 and 15,000 doors a year. Alan Etkin photo.

that is essentially unstable—would have very severe ramifications not only for our members but also for the communities in the interior.

"If your suggestion is that 50 percent of the wood is going to end up in value-added products and secondary manufacturing, that's patently impossible. There aren't the markets there to do that, and there never will be. *We will never reach the day when 50 percent of BC's wood products are in secondary products.*" (emphasis added)

Unstable—or unable?

Ultimately Evans's committee didn't agree with Scoffield. Quite the opposite, the committee unanimously decided to place its faith in the "unstable" companies to which Scoffield referred. The data simply didn't support the claim that remanufacturers were inherently risky businesses. During the bleak 1991–92 recessionary period, for instance, remanufacturing companies posted better financial performances than the province's major forest companies, losing only 1.7 percent on assets compared to the industry average loss of 5.5 percent. And while pay in the remanufacturing sector wasn't as high as the industry average of $53,700, it was still a respectable $35,000.

But perhaps the most telling statistic unearthed by the politicians related to job creation. On average, the committee found it took half a million board feet of lumber production to keep just one job going in today's highly automated sawmills. In the value-added wood products industry, that same amount of wood created a little more than 4.5 full-time jobs. That is, for the same volume of wood, value-added mills generated about $160,000 in total wages compared to $53,000 in the sawmill. And these are extra new jobs and wages, because remanufacturers get the lumber after other companies have run it through their sawmills.

Despite all this, time and again the committee heard bad news. During hearings in Victoria, Ladysmith, Comox, New Westminster, Penticton, Revelstoke, Kamloops, Castlegar, Williams Lake, Smithers and Prince George, the remanufacturers (or remanners as they're called in the industry) complained about the serious obstacles they faced in running successful businesses. A lack of access to lumber produced by the majors was cited most often, followed closely by the unwillingness of financial institutions to support value-added mills that didn't have a guaranteed supply of raw material, let alone the equity that the majors can pledge from their Crown tenure holdings. No timber. No money. As Gian Sandhu, a Williams Lake remanufacturer told Evans and his fellow committee members: "Remanufacturers are probably required more than any other business to put up a security. That makes it very tough for people like us who have invested close to $3 million in a project. You're looking to make it viable, and you don't see it happening....Bankers obviously are emphasizing that unless you have timber allocated to your company, the banking institution will not come with open hands to assist you."

For Evans, this was probably the most baffling information he'd confront during the many hours he listened to remanufacturers. How could smart business people with good ideas, people who wanted to work with wood and create new jobs, have so much trouble accessing it? "Here in British Columbia, where the wood is all around us, where the timber on our front lawn is two and a half feet across, it boggles the mind that the biggest impediment to businesses would be that they can't get access to wood," Evans said. When Scoffield was confronted with evidence of the majors refusing to supply lumber to remanners unless they had standing timber of their own to offer in return, he lamely replied: "I don't particularly have a comment to make....Certainly the story you portray is true in some cases; it's not true in others."

More From Less
Comparison of Jobs to Timber Harvested

Sawmills

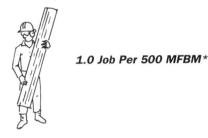

1.0 Job Per 500 MFBM*

Value-Added Average

4.55 Jobs Per 500 MFBM*

* MFBM means thousands of board feet measure, which is the equivalent of 1,000 feet in length by 1 foot in width by 1 inch in thickness.

Source: Select Standing Committee on Forests, Energy, Mines and Petroleum Resources, Lumber Remanufacturing in British Columbia (1993).

Timber takeback

Throughout the hearings, the major companies opposed extending the timber quota to remanners, but failed to offer much by way of alternatives. So the Evans committee, not surprisingly, identified tenure reform as a major theme. Indeed, some committee members felt strongly that the majors should be made to give back half their Crown-granted timber-cutting rights. The final report issued on June 3, 1993 fell well short of that, but carried the imprimatur of all committee members who were anxious to clear away the impediments to a vital new part of the forest industry. At the time of the report's release about 12,000 workers were employed in 565 value-added mills across the province. The committee endorsed doubling the number of jobs in the sector by the year 2000, with a further doubling by 2010. They believed that with the right policy changes there could be 20,000 to 25,000 direct jobs in the value-added sector by the year 2000, and roughly 50,000 by 2010. Using standard in-dustry multipliers of two indirect jobs created for every direct forestry job, the value-added sector alone could support up to 150,000 British Columbians by the year 2010. These totals are just approximations, and may be opti-mistic. But they suggest on the manu-facturing side what we have already seen on the logging and financial sides— that huge opportunities await us in the new value economy.

One of these opportunities is the offsetting of forest industry job losses as remanufacturing expands and new protected areas are announced by the provincial government. "One way out of the box that we're in would be to do everything possible to extract every job in the forest, then in the sawmill and then in the remanufacturing plant from every stick that we harvest," Evans said. "If we were prepared to do that in an aggressive fashion, it's my belief you could experience 12-percent withdrawals...almost without notice." This strategy is pivotal to resolving wilderness conflicts. But it will also help offset the impact of reducing logging levels to compensate for past overcutting and overproduction, and to make way for more sustainable forest practices in the future.

To meet these growth goals, the Evans committee endorsed doubling the cut allocated under the Ministry of Forests' small business program to remanufacturers from the present 5 percent of the total AAC, and increase the allocation by 1 percent per year over five years. Perhaps even more significant, all timber recovered by the Crown as a result of changes in com-pany ownership would be directed to the same program. Not surprisingly, the report was quickly condemned by both the Council of Forest Industries and by the International Woodworkers of America, whose outcries may go some way to explaining why the recommendations have yet to be implemented. In its place, the Forest Renewal Plan has earmarked between $20 million and $40 million a year for assistance to the value-added sector through backing or topping up commercial loans to new companies, and assisting in the research and development of new products. The Plan states as a prime objective "to ensure that those who are

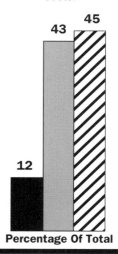

The Small Not The Tall

Small businesses dominate the Reman sector

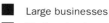

Percentage Of Total

- ■ Large businesses
- ▨ Medium businesses
- ▨ Small businesses

Source: Jim McWilliams, Structure and Significance of the Value-Added Wood Products Industry in British Columbia (FRDA Report #203, 1993).

For want of wood

Basically about five years ago I wanted to build a reman centre in central Vancouver Island. I spent a large amount of money—in excess of $50,000—on drawings and consultants' fees, and I went to the majors to get some form of guaranteed wood supply. They wanted us to build it, but they wouldn't put anything in writing to us. We had a number of meetings with them, and in the end they would not sign any guarantees.

When I went to the bank to build this remanufacturing plant, the bank would not give the funds I required because I couldn't give them a guaranteed log or wood supply. I think there's a real market for it...I was born and raised in Lake Cowichan, and I've seen what has happened to that area. I think a reman mill could go in there. But a person going in there and spending the money has to have a log supply or some type of wood supply. Mills are shutting down. There's one large mill left there, and they're on the verge of shutting down....

We had all the contracts; we just didn't have them signed. We took the contracts—because we had verbal assurances that we were going to get a certain amount of log or cant supply—and we went to the banks with that. But because they weren't signed, they said no. We were borrowing $6 million, so it was a lot of money to the banks. They needed the assurance that we would have a wood supply. That's the only thing that stopped it. There were 60 jobs there, and it was a very modern mill.

Gordon Carlson, quoted in Report of Proceedings of the Select Standing Committee on Forests, Energy, Mines and Petroleum Resources (Issue 8, Ladysmith, January 12, 1993).

willing to do more with the public's timber—particularly those looking to create more jobs per cubic metre processed—have greater access to the wood they require." The objective is laudable, but it raises a troubling question. The greatest collateral a value-added company could ask for is a secure supply of timber. And legislated changes that give them access to that offer the greatest security that future supplies will be there.

The mantra of "value-added"

Corky Evans wasn't the first to champion the benefits of shifting from a volume-based to a value-oriented industry. Indeed, "value-added" has become the popular mantra of the future. It is spoken in many voices—it's the move from cost minimization to value maximization, from reactive opportunism to strategic planning, from mass production to niche marketing. But being everything to all people, this phrase—like sustainable development—is suspect. Our definition of the value economy is very specific: in the woods it means a much-reduced cut and a new forest stewardship that lives off nature's interest not its capital. In the market it means getting the highest dollar value. But on the manufacturing side, value-added doesn't just mean any processing that improves the product in the customer's eyes, such as wrapping lumber in plastic and thus increasing profits. It means much more.

In recent years, major forest products firms have recognized the need to add value to what they produce, and have made important strides. For example, Canadian Forest Products Ltd. runs Canfor Specialty, a south Vancouver mill that employs 30 people who re-cut lumber into valuable window stock. The company and the woodworkers union, IWA–Canada, have reached a special contract agreement covering the mill that provides wages ranging from $12 to $18 an hour, compared to the master agreement covering most sawmills on BC's coast where union workers receive wages of between $18 and $23 an hour. The union has agreed to the concessions to keep workers in the local, whose membership has declined from 5,000 a decade ago to 2,500 today.

Elsewhere in the Lower Mainland, MacMillan Bloedel Ltd. employs over 120 people making Parallam, a specialized engineered wood product with unique strength characteristics. The product is made from adhering wood strands together to form a product that is touted as being as strong as steel. Given the likely closure or downsizing of many BC pulp mills due to an increased demand for recycled content and a decreasing global need for wood pulp, more fibre could become available for producers of products like Parallam. Engineered wood products producers could also be the beneficiaries of some of the fibre coming out of our second-growth forests, a nice fit with the commercial thinning of second-growth forests discussed in Chapter 6.

These are but two examples of a gradual shift in thinking on the part of BC's major forest products companies. Can the majors move faster? Big companies have an established way of doing business, and an established product line and customer base. As a rule, they tend to shy away from trying to penetrate niche

The missing page 30

In the event that these recommendations are not strong enough, or major licensees do not respond in a positive manner to the co-operative environment the Committee has created, the following alternative recommendations could be implemented:

1. Enact the recommendations of the Forest Resources Commission and reduce timber allocated to licensees to 50% of its present level.

2. Create a Crown corporation to sell timber, and make social considerations a function of sale.

3. Buy a major licensee and use it to feed remanufacturing facilities around the province.

4. Place a duty on the export of low-quality commodities.

5. Place inspectors in pulp mills and sawmills to stop useable solid wood from being chipped.

6. Require anyone selling wood products outside British Columbia to have a permit. Create an export council of permit holders. Charge the council with setting minimum prices for all commodities sold per year. Require that anyone meeting that price in British Columbia have the right of first refusal.

7. Make it an offence for any broker of wood to refuse to sell unsold inventory to a legitimate buyer for cash.

Page 30, removed from a legislative committee report just before going to press. Select Standing Committee on Forests, Energy, Mines and Petroleum Resources, *Lumber Remanufacturing in British Columbia: First Report* (1993).

markets. "The tenured companies, historically, have been volume producers," says Colin Harte, a member of the Independent Lumber Remanufacturers Association (ILRA) and head of Uneeda Wood Products, a custom remanufacturing company. "They're used to selling volumes of wood. And this is a mindset that has been there for years and years. And it's still there....The tenured companies are more inclined to do commodity-type value-adding. You might take some material and kiln-dry it and grade it, and at that point you've added value." Then the slightly modified product is shipped to some other country where another company does the real value-added work. In contrast to the majors, BC remanners necessarily buy small amounts of wood, and have a specific end use in mind. "A small company or an entrepreneur is going to be buying in much smaller quantities. Therefore, he is more inclined, he has to deal with, those niche markets. He can't get into the volume market."

JOB CREATION   **BUSINESS·**

NDP tree harvest plan angers union

GORDON HAMILTON
Sun Business Reporter

A legislative proposal to create more jobs from B.C.'s timber harvest has riled unionized woodworkers who fear any new jobs will be

We all know we are going to be losing a lot of timber because of environmental regulations

THOMAS MANESS

he said, will not necessarily come at expense of large companies or unionized workers.

The attacks have puzzled industry observers because both the IWA and COFI support development of value-added manufacturing

MB on value added

In fact, anything that adds worth to the product in the eyes of your customer is part of the value-added process....

To some people, adding value in the forest industry really means remanufacturing, or manufacturing of finished products. They believe that unless you take wood farther along the path to becoming a finished product—by cutting it into components that can be used to make products like window stock, or better still, by actually manufacturing the finished windows—you really aren't adding value.

Generally, this view sees value-added manufacturing as a labour-intensive activity promising new jobs in an industry where the traditional employment base is eroding. Responsibility for creating those new "value-added" jobs is often put at the doorstep of the large companies. When they don't take such initiatives, companies are sometimes accused of lack of vision, lack of initiative, or over-eagerness to make profits "the easy way".

...Successful value-added investment is based on a wide range of considerations such as market demand, competitive position, and sustainability. New jobs may, and often do, come when those investments result in a profitable venture. But to pursue value-added *primarily* because it will create jobs is to put the cart before the horse. It invites endeavours that are likely to founder in the competitive rigours of the marketplace, so that any new employment will be short-lived.

...In some cases, investment in value-added is a direct source of new jobs. In others, it preserves jobs by saving operations facing collapse. In still others, it may actually reduce jobs by introducing a higher level of plant automation.

But in every case, the goals are the same: *to improve the value of recovery from the forest resource and to improve the company's competitiveness in domestic and world markets.*

MacMillan Bloedel Ltd., "Adding Value to the Forest," in *Forest Perspectives* (December 1991).

The move to value

In the quest to do more with our wood there is an essential role for commodity lumber mills because not all value-added producers or remanufacturers have the equipment or the desire to make their products from raw logs: many prefer to have somebody else do the initial milling. But getting the primary sawmills to think in terms of being the first link in a chain of value-added production won't be easy, says Evans. "The primary industry considers itself a commodity lumber producer that recovers value-added products from this operating process, as opposed to an industry that produces primarily value-added with only the fall-down going into commodities." To turn this around requires harnessing the power of the primary mills in a new value-added strategy that starts in the forest where trees are carefully selected for logging. It then moves to the log yard where our wooden diamonds are meticulously sorted by species and grade. After the sort, the logs move to the auction block where the highest price

Jean Larrivee, president of Larrivee Guitars, holds one of fifteen guitars made daily at his East Vancouver shop. In business since 1968, Larrivee has built up a steady and faithful clientele of guitarists around the world. Most Larrivee guitar tops are made of top quality BC Sitka spruce logs which Larrivee personally inspects and buys from booms on the Fraser River. He's been known to pay up to $7,000 for a single log, but then each fine guitar turned out of his shop retails for $1,640 to $6,400. Larrivee employs a staff of thirty. Steve Bosch photo.

is fetched for the wood. And it ends in any one of a number of mills where the best possible products are extracted. All these activities are carefully linked by an understanding that value comes first.

The primary producers still resist this sort of treatment of our wood. For example, there's the bias against Interior lumber. The Evans committee found a "prevalent" bias among sawmillers that only 10 to 20 percent of local wood has value-added potential, even though some companies were getting 50 percent value-added from their timber supply. Charles Merriam of Cherryville, a small sawmiller, understands this when he sees one of his neighbours making shakes from bug-killed pine, and another using bug-killed white pine with blister rust to make cants for veneer stocks. Merriam himself processes small-dimension cedar which he sells to remanners who make panels. Unfortunately, these specialty mills are the exception to the rule today. In the Cherryville of the 1950s, there were as many as twenty sawmills, Merriam says. "There's three of us now."

Still, commodity lumber has a place. Keith Wyton, president of the Port Alberni cedar garden furniture maker, Sarita Furniture Ltd., says remanufacturers want pre-cut boards which they can then re-cut to rigid specifications. "We need to make sure we maintain a sufficient sawmilling industry which will then supply the next step with the raw materials to make the value-added component." But Wyton is also aware that the social benefits that were supposed to flow from the timber licences that supplied mills built by the likes of MacMillan Bloedel, haven't been maintained. "The problem is from a society point of view that fewer and fewer people are seeing the benefits. People are factored out of the production process by technology. From a straight business point of view MB is doing the right thing. But that only flies as long as we let them use the public's resource."

Three studies in value

Given the need to curb logging levels and reduce consumption, the "sufficient" sawmilling sector Wyton mentions must be a lot smaller in the future than it is today. The trick lies in redirecting the most lumber possible to sawmills that can respond to the needs of those most capable of adding value.

Wyton's company, for example, makes twenty-five different products including benches, tables and chairs, all made from western red cedar. The products require only about five minutes' assembly work when the customer takes them home. To date, Sarita has purchased all its wood on the open market, much of it from MB. And it's a successful business. "We've been in business for five years. We've been exporting for about four years serious production volumes, mostly to Europe," Wyton says. The company currently employs 10 to 12 people full-time year-round. The wages range from $12 to $14 an hour in addition to a benefits package that includes dental, disability and life insurance. "We're much more interactive with the material in our operation," Wyton says. "In sawmills you look at the material rather than touching it as it goes by you. You look for defects and pull them out. In our business people do a lot of different things, there's a lot more variety." In a given year, Sarita will require about 250,000 board feet of lumber to sustain its production, that's less than 25,000 board feet per employee, way below the amount needed in the commodity lumber mill.

Gian Sandhu's remanufacturing company in Williams Lake is much bigger, employing about 50 people. He pays an average hourly wage of $18, 70 percent of the IWA rate. His lumber too is supplied by a local sawmill, Lignum Ltd., and his workers re-cut Lignum's wood into a wide array of products including door jambs, brick moulds, furniture components and components for the Japanese housing market. Sandhu describes his work force as happy and versatile. "Some people, I've had working for me for over twelve years," he says. "They wouldn't

Gerry Sillers, partner at B.W. Creative Wood Industries Ltd., displays some of his company's ready-to-sell stairway posts. Steve Bosch photo.

go work for anybody else." In a given year, Sandhu requires about 20 million board feet of lumber to operate his company at peak capacity. This may sound like a lot of wood, and it is. But to support one job at Jackpine requires only 39 percent of the wood needed to create one full-time job in Williams Lake's highly automated, low-labour commodity sawmills.

Far to the south of Sandhu's mill in the Lower Mainland, Gerry Sillers oversees the operation of an even larger company, B.W. Creative Wood Industries Ltd. The partner and financial controller of the company has a fluctuating workforce of 70 to 80 workers. "We bring in rough green lumber, you know, two-by-fours in various species —hemlock, pine and cedar—and we cut it up. We remanufacture that wood into turning squares, and we then make spindles, posts and railings—stairway components. It's highly merchandised, shrink-wrapped. And 80 percent of what we do is exported into the US," Sillers says. "In terms of value-added, we are probably adding as much value as anybody." The wood required to sustain these 70-plus jobs each year? About 3.6 million board feet, or 50,000 board feet per person.

These are but three companies successfully re-cutting wood in BC's remanufacturing sector. The companies are all very different, but collectively they consume 23.9 million board feet of lumber a year and employ a combined work force of about 135 full-time people. By comparison, Lignum Ltd., Jackpine's main supplier, produces about 177 million board feet of lumber and employs 200 people. To sustain one job at Lignum requires 885,000 board feet of production. The three remanufacturing mills use only an eighth as much wood as Lignum, but with it, they provide two-thirds as many jobs.

WoodNet

WoodNet is a network of small to medium-sized wood products manufacturers on Washington's Olympic Peninsula. Testing concepts pioneered in Europe, WoodNet helps member firms tap new markets, cooperate when it serves their interest, and stretch the region's dwindling wood supply. Today, WoodNet's membership exceeds 300 individuals and firms. They make a wide range of items, from construction and marine products to home furnishings, arts and crafts, garden products, and kitchen wares. A non-profit corporation, WoodNet's board of directors is currently composed of owners and directors of nine member firms....

WoodNet has arranged for business owners to tour each other's shops.

Managers who had been neighbours for years often found that one made—or could make—what the other needed. WoodNet has also helped to establish regular meetings of firms with similar products and markets. Groups of artisans, remanufacturing firms, cabinetmakers, and others have formed, creating forums for business ideas. Acting together, firms can reduce their costs for materials, professional services, and marketing. They can also gain access to larger markets by jointly manufacturing products no small firm could supply alone.

Kirk Johnston, *Beyond Polarization: Emerging Strategies for Reconciling Community and the Environment* (Seattle WA: University of Washington, Northwest Policy Center, 1993).

Diversity within and without

Instead of channelling more wood into the hands of people like Wyton, Sandhu and Sillers, today's commodity lumber mills continue to ship wood that is worked over and over again by remanufacturers in the US, in the bustling economy of the Pacific Rim or in Europe. In BC's interior alone, about 75 or 80 percent of our general lumber ends up in US markets, Sandhu told the Evans committee. And Evans believes that at most half of that wood ends up in the construction industry, the rest going to remanufacturers abroad. Whatever the actual number is, a staggering amount of wood is leaving BC in grossly undermanufactured form, the employment and revenue values to be captured elsewhere.

Ironically, the American states that process that wood report much the same thing happening to their own wood. Many remanufacturers in the US Pacific Northwest are wholly dependent on BC old-growth, yet the region's big forest companies export some 40 percent of their lumber as raw logs to Japan and other Pacific Rim countries. In a recent study of small industry owners in Oregon, "participants estimated that between 50 percent and 90 percent of the remanufacturable wood stock produced in Oregon leaves the state in primary product form." The major losers in this are workers in the US Pacific Northwest and here in BC as our primary product goes from us to the US to replace their wood, which goes from the US out. And the major beneficiary is Japan, the most organized and successful economic competitor on earth. We pay the price twice, first when we relinquish the raw resource, and second when we buy back the finished product.

Evans and many other people around BC want to change the linear, one-way road we're on. To do so means diversifying production, just as we speed the process of changing our approach to forest stewardship. We need, in quick order, a reduction in primary sawmilling capacity and a corresponding rise in labour-intensive secondary woodworking. We need to create a situation where the industry is primarily value-added, where the big players gear production to suit the needs of the smaller players, where the whole industry and everybody in it takes the log as far along as possible in the production process. Ultimately, this is a joint effort involving a mix of players. But it's a far different mix than what we have today.

Encouraging diversity won't be easy, but it is vital in a province where so much economic activity revolves around one industry, and a limited aspect of it at that. A recent survey of 385 remanufacturing companies found 66 percent were located in the Vancouver Forest Region, the bulk of them in the Lower Mainland. The next biggest concentration, 20 percent, was in the Kamloops Forest Region, home to the booming Okanagan district. For smaller timber-dependent communities in the north and east of the province the lesson is simple. They can continue to turn their logs and rough-cut lumber over to other regions to process or they can begin to develop local business in which more people work with wood closer to where it is logged. In Quesnel, for example, over the past fifteen years there has been a one-third increase in cut levels, with

Flexible manufacturing networks

Flexible manufacturing networks are groups of two or more independent firms that collaborate to some degree in order to compete more effectively in larger markets. Network cooperation takes many forms, from exchange of information to joint ventures for product development and marketing. The key to cooperation is that firms pool selected resources to achieve outcomes that are not possible if they act in isolation. In the Emilia–Romagna district in Northern Italy, large numbers of networks exist among very small firms to exploit the complementarities among their combined product lines....In Denmark, networks of similar furniture companies have been formed to invest in large scale facilities such as lacquering plants that the members could not afford individually. Also, the Danish government has a three year, $18 million dollar program underway to stimulate network formation for small manufacturing firms to prepare them for the competitive challenges of the European internal market after the end of 1992.

Northwest Policy Center, *Improving the Vitality of Oregon's Secondary Wood Products Sector*, report for the Oregon Interim Legislative Committee on Forest Policy (Seattle WA: University of Washington, 1990).

no net job growth. Meanwhile, the number of unemployment insurance recipients increased by 95 percent in Quesnel, and by 105 percent in Williams Lake. Without forestry-related economic diversification many towns across BC will suffer a similarly rapid decline in prosperity, and a continuous outflow of residents and resources.

"What we're seeing outside the Lower Mainland," says Mike Tarr of Prince Rupert, "is the disappearance of a whole bunch of people that aren't going to be here for much longer because their jobs are going to go. And unless there's some ability at the local level or the regional level to bring in alternative industries that are probably still going to be resource-loaded and dependent, then we'll see, over the next ten or twenty years, a massive shift out of the north and out of the eastern part of the province into the larger metropolitan areas."

Wood culture

To stave off that exodus requires opening up opportunities to work in the woods and in more labour-intensive value-added mills. But a strategy for enhancing the prospects of the province's forest-based rural communities goes well beyond that. It must take advantage of the much broader range of values which the natural forest has to offer. In Germany, for example, people both romanticize the forest and cherish what comes from it. They surround themselves with the feel and texture of wood. But in BC, where people are surrounded by trees, the natural forest and its wood products are both often treated with disdain, a source of mere commodity products, and a paycheque. In his home town of Port Alberni, Keith Wyton says it would be quite possible to support a millwork operation that made wood frame windows for the town. "But here we use plastic and aluminum." The same indifference to building materials reigns in Prince George, gateway to BC's northern forests and home to some of the biggest wood processing facilities in the province. As he rushes from his office to meet some Japanese tourists arriving on an airplane, Greg Jadrzyk, an executive with COFI's Prince George office, says he already knows one of the first questions he'll be asked. "They'll ask me to see some BC wood buildings, they always do," he says. "And I'll tell them, `Go look in Japan'. I would love to take them to see wood, but there's just not much to see here. Except for the Native people who are really into it with their longhouses, and some schools."

Temple of timber. A post-and-beam house by Paul Merrick Architects graphically displays an appreciation for BC wood using custom-milled western red cedar.
Danny Singer (Animotion Inc.) photo.

Perhaps one way to start valuing wood in the forest industry is to value it more in our everyday experience—build with it, showcase it, marvel at its beauty. The Canadian Wood Council in Ottawa certainly does, and it's not just for philosophical reasons. The Council sees a dramatic potential for the use of wood in low-rise commercial and small office buildings, high-value wood used in local markets with local labour. Similarly, the BC forest research institute, Forintek, produces studies showing wood to be cost-competitive with steel and concrete in small commercial buildings. But in Prince George, Jadrzyk and others from the industry faced a huge battle to get any wood at all showcased in the new University of Northern British Columbia, despite the immediate benefits to local woodworkers and carpenters to say nothing of the warm atmosphere created for students and staff. At the time, the provincial government's own BC Building

Corporation, which constructs many public buildings, had no guidelines in place giving preferential treatment to wood products. Expanded opportunities for domestic and exportable wood frame architecture and construction could be a big boon to the industry, opening a huge new market for wood products and skilled trades. "A lot of the market is right here where you can produce small runs and small quantities of very customer-specific products," says Roger Ennis, a respected industry analyst with BC Trade.

Hand in hand with valuing our wood more in our built environment is valuing the landscape from which it comes. There is a great range of values in our natural landscape, economic and spiritual values that are growing all the time as wild places around the world disappear. But in BC the full economic potential of wilderness tourism and outdoor recreation remains untapped, largely because so much of the land is controlled by those who are hooked on the drive to vol-ume and who will block local tourism initiatives that compete for the same land. Despite widespread clearcutting, tourist visits to BC's parks and wilderness areas continue to climb. Quotas have even been established in many areas because our parks cannot handle visitor demand. Here again, the development of this potential is held in check by the tenures that overlay the landscape, and by government policies that go fast on forest "development" but slow on any other uses that might conflict with logging.

This inertia is sadly out of step. Of its own accord, the economy is rapidly moving to take advantage of non-exploitive values in the natural forest. Overall, between 1981 and 1991 jobs in resource extraction and manufacturing fell from 153,000 to 113,400. Meanwhile, the economy grew by 213,000 jobs. While resource jobs fell by 20 percent, the service sector, including tourism, grew by 60 percent. Services accounted for $45 billion in the provincial economy, while the total goods sector was only $18 billion. One service industry is repeatedly cited, from Revelstoke to Tofino, as the alternative to forestry dependence: tourism. The arguments are well-worn, especially the greater number of jobs in this industry than in forestry (180,000 vs. 86,600), many of which are in the small business sector. As forestry declines, tourism is one of the service sector's top growth industries, averaging almost 6 percent growth per year from 1981 to 1991. In the next decade, it is predicted to expand 50 percent faster than other businesses, and to provide 50 percent more jobs than the BC average.

All the rebuttals are well-worn too: that these are often lower paying or seasonal jobs; that the overall financial contribution of forestry is still greater; that tourism doesn't "produce" anything. But the positive economic indicators of BC's growing SuperNatural tourism industry are dramatic. In the Alberni-Clayoquot region, for example, Tofino land values are well ahead of those in the nearby logging town of Ucluelet. Economic development officers in Port Alberni

Wood building with green qualities

Forintek's new Western Laboratory has been rewarded for its energy-efficient design, cited for its 25 percent cost-savings compared to conventional steel construction and applauded for its aesthetic features. Together, the Forintek Laboratory and the companion FERIC facility demonstrate the potential for designing modern wood buildings to meet stringent maintenance, noise, vibration, energy efficiency and functional criteria as well as all applicable fire and structural codes. In short, the Forintek–FERIC complex attests to the competitive advantages of wood in a commercial and light industrial construction market previously dominated by structural steel and concrete.

...Embodied energy represents one area where wood building materials have a distinct sustainable development advantage over steel materials...the use of steel building materials in place of wood in the Forintek laboratory would result in the use of three times as much energy.

Water use represents another area where wood has a distinct environmental advantage over steel...the wood design requires only a small fraction of the water used for the steel design. In fact about 85% of the water used in the wood design is actually accounted for by the steel fasteners.

...carbon dioxide emissions for steel are more than three and a half times greater than for wood.

People are rightfully concerned that wood products entail serious environmental consequences in terms of the number of trees harvested and the attendant effects on natural forest environments. But the results presented here suggest the potential for environmental gains from using wood instead of steel in terms of energy and water use as well as atmospheric emissions and solid waste.

Forintek Canada Corp. and Wayne B. Trusty & Associates Limited, "Forintek's Western Laboratory: Building in Wood to Meet Environmental Objectives" (1991).

attest that one reason this pulp and paper town on the way to Tofino is staying afloat after the disastrous layoffs in the 1980s is because of tourists passing through town on the way to visit Clayoquot Sound and Long Beach, and from retirees moving into the area to take advantage of its natural amenities. A region's ability to provide such amenities is fast becoming a key to attracting capital and clean investment in the emerging high-tech world, where businesses can pick and choose their home base. And the possibilities don't end there. One background study for the Forest Resources Commission came to the surprising conclusion that of a sample of 55 communities, 14 were primarily dependent on pension revenues from retirees. In this competition of amenities, a healthy environment translates into a healthy economy. Proximity to designated parks is a proven direct stimulus to local economic diversity and community well-being.

Forintek's University of BC headquarters is a dramatic but sadly rare study in the use of wood in commercial-scale architecture. Simon Scott photo.

As BC struggles to make the transition to a new forest economy and a new wood culture that values the forest in all its manifestations, the issue is not what industry counts most, but how a diversity of industries can happily coexist. To ensure that this coexistence is possible demands a commitment to a larger transition.

A NEW INDUSTRIAL STRATEGY

I T WAS A REMARKABLE ADMISSION, COMING AS IT DID FROM THE president of British Columbia's second-largest forest company. At what was later described as an informal dinner, Fletcher Challenge Canada Ltd. president, Doug Whitehead, told then Forests Minister, Dan Miller, his company was prepared to relinquish control of some of its vast timber holdings, and to "explore the possibilities" of shifting some Crown timber rights to community or aboriginal interests. The statement was all the more remarkable coming from a company that just a few years earlier had sought a 5.23-million-hectare tree farm licence in the Mackenzie region. The application had triggered a massive outpouring of public opposition to forest policy in the province and later scuttled government plans to roll vast areas of public forest into corporate tree farm licences.

Whitehead had ascended to the top echelons of Fletcher Challenge Canada Ltd. after the company lost its bid in the Mackenzie region, and he had witnessed a sharp rise in public distrust of his forest company and others. People from all walks of life including truck loggers, Native leaders, community economic development officers and environmental activists, were clamouring for changes in provincial forest policy, and tenure reform was at the top of the list. So, as Whitehead and Miller ate, the company president told the cabinet minister that it was time his company and others acknowledged the need for change and presided over, rather than opposed, a transfer of some timber tenures from large corporations to smaller, local players.

"Society is moving in this direction—we'd better be a part of the solution than a reactionary force against it," Whitehead said, before telling the minister what he already knew: that a handful of companies controlled just under three-quarters of all timber tenures in BC. "Perhaps a better formula would be, in rough numbers, 40 percent big companies, 20 percent communities, 20 percent aboriginal peoples, 10 percent private woodlots and 10 percent small companies," Whitehead said, adding: "There doesn't have to be a net loss of jobs. *In fact, this could stimulate the forest sector by bringing in new players with new ideas* (emphasis added)...I believe we have to shake free of some of the old concepts that have steered our industry for so long. By exercising less control over the resource we will gain public support. To break the impasse we have been at over the last decade we all need to think differently and take some risks."

Smaller tenure holders and a competitive log market

A bigger share of the Allowable Annual Cut should be allocated to smaller tenure holders who will manage the forests with emphasis on such values as community watersheds, range, wildlife, recreation and community forests. In essence, the Commission sees a tenure system that significantly reduces the volume of timber now controlled by a relatively small number of large corporations and transfers that freed-up volume to the development of a competitive log market.

Forest Resources Commission, *The Future of Our Forests* (1991).

Opposite: The Kitlope River estuary; Myron Kozak photo. Inset: One of the first advertisements in the Super, Natural campaign showing a landscape British Columbia is renowned for, yet is increasingly difficult to find. BC Ministry of Small Business, Tourism and Culture.

"Model T" tenure system

The present system requires an overhaul. What we have here is the Model T tenure system trying to compete with the latest Corvette....

Let us get away from the short term, political and industrial planning to which we have become accustomed. Let us visualize where we want to be in 100 or 200 years—and go for it....I think that the ownership spread we see in Scandinavia has considerable merit, with a balance that creates competition, stewardship, environmental awareness and involvement of people in resource use and management. It is not totally correct for us and I suggest that we should aim for about one third of the productive forest being owned by the Crown, about one third by the major companies, and the balance split evenly between small woodlots and community forests.

Peter Sanders, paper presented as part of a panel discussion titled "Tenure and the Future". Reprinted in *Truck Logger* (February–March 1990).

What if what we are doing is wrong?

What we see in BC is the worst possible scenario in terms of what economists call a command and control economy. I think part of the problem is the monolithic management of the Ministry of Forests. 95 percent of the land base is publicly owned. That means, in essence, that we're getting management which shows no diversity at all. What if the Ministry is wrong? What if what we are doing is wrong? It's the only game in town. We simply do not have the diversity of objectives, the diversity of management philosophies which many of our competitors have. And I think there is a real danger in this. Many countries in the world, including the former Soviet Union and others, have realized the problems one can get into in this type of central planning situation.

David Haley, Faculty of Forestry, UBC, *Seminar proceedings of Determining Timber Supply & Allowable Cuts in BC* (Vancouver, March 1993).

There will always be differences of opinion over what constitutes the right mix of timber holdings, with each special interest trying to stack the deck in its favour. So the numbers proposed by Whitehead and others are not the issue. What is, is the idea of a mix of holdings itself, something BC sorely lacks today. For the health of the province's forests and forestry-dependent communities, a diverse mix must be created so that a lot more people can play a direct role in forest management.

Renouncing the old tenures

In their day, large corporate tenures may have been a reasonable basis for provincial economic development. But as Graham Morgan and other unemployed mill workers in Gitwangak attest, that day has passed. Today's large corporate tenures, reminiscent of the state-backed holdings of the old Soviet Union, concentrate power in the hands of a select, powerful and seemingly unaccountable few. As the resource base is exhausted in the corporate drive for volume, the majors regularly truck logs by mothballed mills and stagnating communities with little regard for the social dislocation they've wrought.

With the demise of the old appurtenance clauses that linked tenure to the maintenance of specific mills, companies can dispose of wood as they see fit. And more often than not that means running it through mega-mills in manufacturing centres far away from where the trees come down. The demise of appurtenance is a significant if overlooked development: it means the contractual underpinning of the tenure system is gone. Companies are freed of their contractual constraints. But so too should be government. It is time for what we call the legitimate renunciation of those old tenures to make way for something new.

Such a prescription will trigger dire warnings about massive compensation packages running into the hundreds of millions of dollars. But here there is a lot of smoke and fire. A significant amount of tenure can, in fact, be taken away from corporations with little if any financial compensation. Under existing legislation huge amounts of timber can be taken out of Timber Supply Areas and reallocated, over time, to new players. Between five and ten years from now 157 volume-based forest licences—95 percent of all such agreements—come up for renewal, and the government is under no obligation to renew the licences.

In these TSAs, the government also has other powers of even more immediate consequence. It can order reductions in logging levels through timber supply reviews that bring down the level to whatever is deemed sustainable. Significant reductions have been ordered already, and more are promised in the months and years ahead. The government can do the same wherever it seeks to prevent damage to environmentally sensitive or unique areas. Together, these reductions could be of a sizable magnitude, but in neither case would they entail a duty to compensate.

At stake here is a huge amount of land and timber—in fact, the majority of "working forest" in BC, which currently supplies more than 44 million cubic metres, or 1.27 million truckloads of logs per year to BC's sawmills and pulp mills. The opportunity is obvious: all or a portion of all the major corporate tenure holders can be phased out of timber supply areas without risk of compensation. "You just phase them right out, and phase in other people," says Ken Drushka. All the government has to do is follow its own Forest Act in making the transition. "It's just an act of political will," Drushka says. "The TSA stuff is easy to deal with."

TSAs represent the largest tenure commitment the government currently has. As wood volume is freed up from expired licences, new area-based licences covering small, identifiable parcels of forest land should be allocated to individuals under a vastly expanded woodlot program, to Native bands through the settlement of land claims and to local governments interested in establishing community forests. This is particularly important in second-growth forests where tending on a small scale can begin right away. To forestall this transfer, Drushka says, is to accept the prevailing corporate view of second-growth forests as fibre farms to be cut over every 60 to 80 years for cheap pulp and wood fibre. This reallocation would be particularly desirable for those areas close to small communities. It is time now to search out areas where forest soils are good, where second-growth forests are badly neglected and in need of tending, and where the potential for local processing is high. This process should begin immediately with a formal commitment by government.

The real obstacles lie with the more prized old-growth forests and the tighter contractual undertakings of the Tree Farm Licences (TFLs) which embrace some of the most valuable old-growth forests remaining. Here, government expropriation will undoubtedly trigger calls for daunting compensation packages. However, as recent studies on compensation attest, corporate claims of compensation are sometimes legally unfounded and economically inflated. From the few expropriations that have taken place, highly inflated claims of lost economic opportunities have not resulted in commensurate payments by government. In the case of timber-rich South Moresby Park, for example, where one forest company lost substantial timber cutting rights, the compensation claim soared to $65 million. Yet the actual payment was in the $37-million range. With appropriate legislation setting out a fair process and formula for compensation, the costs could be kept to a reasonable level.

Paying the piper

Governments are naturally resistant to tenure reform because of potential economic repercussions, especially at a time of mounting public debt. But there is a mechanism that allows for compensation without upping the debt: vastly expanded log markets. By using the market, the government can move quickly to complete its promised representative system of protected areas while also freeing up forest land in small, area-based tenures to a host of new players. And, by instituting widespread competitive timber sales, the whole venture can be self-financing.

This, says Mike Major, was the opportunity lost by the now-besieged NDP government almost the day it came into office. At that time, Fletcher Challenge was in the process of selling its massive timber holdings on south Vancouver Island and two Lower Mainland sawmills to Interfor. This neat move allowed Fletcher to pocket about $65 million while avoiding the headache of logging in the hotly contested remaining coastal old-growth forests of southern Vancouver Island.

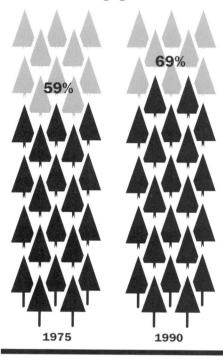

Corporate Control

Corporate control of committed harvesting rights in BC

59% — 1975

69% — 1990

■ Largest 10 Corporations

Source: British Columbia Forest Resources Commission, The Future of Our Forests *(1991).*

What is the piper's pay?

Timber tenure gives holders the right to harvest timber. They do not convey the rights to resource rents. The *Forest Act* provides for payment to the Crown of stumpages, literally the value of the tree on the stump before the application of human effort. However, if the Crown failed to collect all resource rents, this would be reflected in the price a buyer would be willing to pay for harvesting rights. In effect, the difference between the value of the standing timber and anticipated stumpages would be capitalized into the value of the tenure.

The buyer would be purchasing the right to obtain timber below its true value. If stumpages extracted all rents, then tenure would have no more value to a sawmill than the "right" to buy wheat would have to a flour mill. Some observers argue that the existence of tenure values provides *prima facie* evidence that rents are not collected.

Richard Schwindt, *Report of the Commission of Inquiry into Compensation for the Taking of Resource Interests* (1993).

By government standards, $65 million was not a lot of money for what was exchanged and, in any event, the transfer required the approval of the Minister of Forests before it went ahead. In short, suggests Major, the provincial government could have made the purchase itself. With the timber assets, the government would then have been in a strong position to protect much of the Clayoquot area, while redirecting wood to log markets. And the whole venture could have been partly, maybe totally, self-financing. "We could have bought the whole thing back, paid off everybody, liquidated the land base of those two mills," Major says, adding there would have been a substantial amount of timber left over that could have been directed into the Ministry of Forests small business program. In the process, the government would have encouraged new, labour-intensive manufacturers to offset job losses from wilderness set-asides. To do this, it would have had to close down the two sawmills, and buy out existing employees or help them find work in the value-added sector. Much of the buy-out could have been covered by the sale of the mill lands for real estate development. This would also have had the effect of reducing sawmill production which was, and remains, well above sustainable levels. But the strategy goes even further, for the government could then have used part of the freed-up timber holdings as leverage to move other companies with logging rights in the Clayoquot Sound area out of the more contentious spots. There would have been no messy compensation battle.

If all this seems far-fetched, consider again Jim Smith's log yard in Lumby. Suppose for the moment that there was a log market big enough to handle the old-growth coming out of the forests of south Vancouver Island. The logs were carefully sorted by species and grade and then auctioned as they are in the Okanagan. In the first year of operation at Lumby, some Ministry of Forests personnel estimated the log yard would post a profit of $3 million on the sale of 50,000 cubic metres of logs. And this was for smaller diameter interior logs, not the prime, centuries-old wood from BC's coastal old-growth. Furthermore, the volume of wood that Major estimates could have been funnelled off Fletcher Challenge's old tenure into the small business program would have been five times greater than what was sold through the Lumby market, translating at that rate into a $15-million return for the provincial government. If such markets were replicated across Vancouver Island, up and down BC's coast and throughout the Interior, huge pools of new money would be generated.

The community in control

For BC's besieged rural communities, there is a desperate need for such a strategy because it is the key to redirecting economic activity. Our existing forest

---

A legal opinion

Some claims to compensation have been wildly overstated. Public resource use contracts are not the same as private property rights. Government should distinguish claims made on legal rights from those based on fairness. We conclude that government has much wider latitude to make reasonable compensation decisions than corporations have claimed.

...Compensation policy should distinguish between those rights which are absolute "vested rights" and those rights which are contingent on future government approval. Traditional law requires only that compensation be paid for the first. Other rights were acquired with the knowledge that continued government discretion was to be exercised in the larger public interest...

We oppose the full market value approach, which should only apply to full private property rights. We believe that the Crown should not have to buy back its own resources that have not yet been extracted or sold. Where compensation is required for a vested public resource contract, fairness requires only that the investor be restored to its original condition by paying the amount invested, less depreciation, plus interest (except where full market value is less). From this amount, we propose that deductions should be made, in fairness, icluding deductions for any damage that the resource holder has done to other public resources, and for failures to fulfill promises....

We advocate that :
* The public owns the forests of BC, and that the property in these trees does not pass at least until they are cut. No payments should be made for the value of standing timber.
* Royalty and stumpage rates be raised to actual market value (thus eliminating any tenure value) and that monies raised be placed in a Compensation Fund.

G. J. McDade, "Report on Compensation Issues Concerning Protected Areas: A Draft Discussion Paper" (Vancouver: Sierra Legal Defence Fund, 1993).

economy has been subsidized by eroding two broad sources of wealth: natural territory and community. A strategy of so-called "community economic development" challenges this traditional economic thinking by changing the direction of economic activity from a linear, extractive one that robs communities of their raw materials, to a circular, self-sustaining one where people stay in the community to play an active role in nurturing and supporting the local economy. The examples we have seen in the previous chapters—from alternative logging to small business development in remanufacturing and tourism to local finance—share this one attribute. All would strengthen and draw on circular economic activity at the community level. For BC's debt-plagued government, a government faced with the prospect of massive rises in unemployment, welfare and social service costs in resource-dependent communities, developing economic policies that promote long-term community health is the urgent challenge.

After eighteen months of deliberations, much the same conclusion was reached by the Commission on Resource and Environment when it released its long-awaited land use plan for Vancouver Island. "Forests cannot be protected or managed as entities that are radically separate from people, and economies cannot be sustained except as an integrated component of the relationship between people and their environment," CORE said in February 1994. "It is essential, therefore, that measures be identified to ensure that more value and benefits from natural resources flow to surrounding communities, particularly those which are vulnerable as a result of resource dependence."

Tenure reform that returns to communities the control and management of local resources is the obvious place to start. But as recent experiences in Revelstoke show, turning corporate tenure over to community control can't take place in a vacuum.

Revelstoke is the latest community in BC to gain control of its own tree farm licence. A few years ago the major forest company in the region decided to sell its timber assets. The impending sale worried many people in Revelstoke because the community had already suffered big job losses in the forest industry. An outside purchase might only make a bad situation worse. In 1982, the city had a population of more than 10,000 and an unemployment rate of about 8 percent. Four years later, following the closure of a sawmill, the population dropped by 2,000, the unemployment rate hit 25 percent, and more timber began to flow out of the region for processing elsewhere.

"The community was feeling quite bitter that our wood was being shipped out to other communities and our guys were laid off," says Loni Parker, a lifetime resident. So when the opportunity arose to buy part of the local tree farm licence, the sawmills in town put up $1 million and the city put up a matching amount through an electric reserve fund. The city then borrowed another $2 million and, through the Revelstoke Community Forest Corporation, purchased half the northern portion of the old TFL. The sale gave the new corporation a

Third order of government

Local government is one of the three orders of government in Canada. It has been recognized and referred to by the public, provincial and federal governments as such for decades (despite any legal definition to the contrary, this was the accepted view).

Local government is the "first" among governments in terms of public rating of accessibility, responsiveness, accountability, etc.

Yet, the new constitutional proposals now say the three orders are federal, provincial and aboriginal.

Local government, the one that relates most to the day-to-day lives of Canadians, is sent to the constitutional dust-bin.

We must have in British Columbia a clear guarantee that local government is an "order" of government. If Canada can't offer us that, then BC must.

Union of British Columbia Municipalities, *Local Government and the Constitutions* (Richmond, BC, 1991).

Revelstoke, the most recent community in BC to bid on and win the right to manage its own tree farm licence. Al Harvey photo.

logging quota of 96,000 cubic metres per year. Under the agreement, half that wood went to the open market for competitive bid, the other half to the city's three corporate partners: Downie St. Sawmill, Kozek Sawmills Ltd. and Cascade Cedar Products Ltd.

"The community feels quite strongly that we did the right thing," says Parker, a member of the corporation's board of directors. "For communities to actually take control of it, look at it, and be well informed about what they have, gives them great power. Maybe it shouldn't be business as usual any more."

But Parker knows her community faces great challenges. Due to past rates, a dramatic reduction in logging looms. "We're looking at a huge reduction in our annual allowable cut over time," Parker admits. She is concerned about the future of her community and the contribution the forest industry makes to the local economy. But she also knows that industries such as tourism depend on a landscape not devastated by logging. That means the corporation must move with care if interests other than logging are to be served. The problem is whether values like wilderness are compatible with the objectives of a forest corporation that, while rooted in community, is still very much timber-driven.

Revelstoke's Francis Maltby is not on the board but he has watched the workings of the board from the outside. Maltby represents several environmental groups at the regional CORE table, and they would like about 70 percent of the licence area protected from logging. Due to extensive dam construction along the Columbia River, and years of logging in side drainages, old-growth in the Columbia basin has shrunk dramatically, with some bio-geoclimatic zones poorly represented. None of this is factored into the arbitrary logging level established for the new tree farm licence, a licence which simply follows the lines of the old corporate tenure. From a huge land base, TFL 23 was broken apart into smaller parcels with the city of Revelstoke getting a "relatively small proportion" of the sliced pie. Maltby says "it sounds awful" when you talk about taking 70 percent of that land base away. "But if you put it into the perspective of the bio-geoclimatic area, I would suspect it's somewhere in the order of 4 to 7 percent of the total. It's a small percentage when you're looking at it from an ecosystem point of view."

Maltby supports the idea of community forests. But if communities are given old corporate tenures and told to maintain old, unsustainable logging levels, nothing changes. Community forests must be run by boards that represent a diversity of interests in the community. And they can only operate with tough provincial policies in place that set logging, biodiversity and environmental standards. Areas of unique wilderness, recreation and biological significance must first be set aside. Once that is done, communities taking on the difficult task of managing their own forests will come to see the wisdom in ending the old volume-driven approach to forest management in favour of a value-based economy where prospects for long-term employment are high. Once they have the power to set their own logging rates, to run their own log markets and collect rents, communities will be motivated to manage their resources for the long term. With a provincial government dedicated to making a new forest economy work, the avenue to transition is wide open.

Revelstoke's foray into community forest management is not such a new idea. Some two decades ago, the residents of the Slocan Valley in the West Kootenay produced the first provincial plan for forest management at the community level. Still considered a classic in regional planning after all these years, the Slocan Valley Community Forest Management Project emerged from the widely held belief in the region that greater local control would encourage longer-term thinking because of the direct effect decisions had on community sustainability, and because of the easier access to information which should exist at the place where decisions are made. "We believe," noted their report, "that

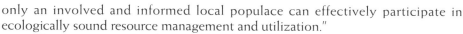

only an involved and informed local populace can effectively participate in ecologically sound resource management and utilization."

There are many details to resolve along the way to community control. For example, establishing the boundaries of community forests is difficult. This is particularly evident in areas of high conflict like Clayoquot Sound. Is Ucluelet, let alone Port Alberni, part of the Clayoquot Sound community? Bordering communities are clearly going to disagree over their interests in the forests, just as residents living far away may wish to have a say in decisions, or at least the process by which decisions are made. There will be differing proposals for the structure of local decision-making bodies, ranging from entirely elected resource boards to appointed representatives bringing different interests to the table. Different circumstances affect different communities and regions. The population density, the extent or remoteness of the forest base, the readiness and desire of the community for self-management, even the state of Native–non-Native relations. As part of an aggressive transition strategy, all these details require new and flexible policies from Victoria.

At root is a single need, however: to give communities the power to manage their own resource base. This power would include the authority to form their own local resource boards which set their own logging levels, allocate logging contracts and woodlot licences, administer provincially approved forest standards, hire and fire community foresters, and monitor the activities of resident silvicultural firms. All this new activity would remain under the watchful eye of a streamlined provincial bureaucracy that is committed to devolving power but that still sets broad guidelines. These are the same communities that are working out their own economic development strategies: where the manufacturing base is strong, a community might choose to direct the flow of wood to local manufacturers. In other more remote locations where forest-tending offers more opportunities, a community might export its unprocessed wood to Vancouver or overseas markets that can return a higher price to local stewards and local resource boards.

Having initiated the shift to Forestopia, having begun to reinvent BC, the challenge for the provincial government is to sustain it, not making an all-or-nothing choice between overweening central control and chaotic community self-determination, but encouraging and balancing the best of the two. Clearly, the pursuit of sustainability cannot be left to COFI or the Ministry of Forests. But neither can the potentially beneficial roles of central agencies be ignored. After all, cut-and-run operators exist at the local level too. Thus, day-to-day local management must be combined with overall provincial legislation that sets out minimum standards for every region, and audits and enforces them. A province-wide land use strategy is needed to coordinate the needs of disparate regions. And finally, the province would have to oversee the shift, both to ensure that communities reinvest their resource rents to sustain local forests, and to protect

Old proposal for a new democracy

That a resource committee, comprised of six local resource management agencies and six local residents, be formed and charged with all resource management within the Slocan Public Sustained Yield Unit, including budgetary responsibilities. Local residents must be Canadian citizens with three years' residency in the Valley....

That a system of "rural woodlots" be instituted within the Slocan PSYU. These will be available to Canadian citizens with three years' residency in the Slocan Valley, and range in size from 10 to 1500 acres. Preference will be given to the Valley walls adjoining inhabited lands. These woodlots would fit into the needs of marginal agricultural communities, protect many of the resources of the Valley bottom, enhance deer habitat, end some of the waste on immature sites, and provide the highest quality and volume of timber possible from these growing sites.

That all stumpage from the Slocan PSYU be reinvested into the Slocan PSYU for at least five years. This time period should be used for the implementation stage of integrated resource management. The money will be allocated by the local resource committee to pay the resource manager and to fund all provincial agencies concerned.

That in order to utilize the decadent cedar, private logs, woodlot logs, and thinnings, a small "product mill" be set up in the Valley. It should produce end products only, from boards to moulding, and serve the local community first....

Slocan Valley Community Forest Management Project, *Final Report*, 2nd ed. (Winlaw, BC, 1976).

Moving money into the future

In rural and small town Canada, the Community Futures program (Department of Employment and Immigration) supports the operation and capitalization of what are known as Business Development Centres. There are 228 BDCs in Canada serving the 2200 medium-sized municipalities (under 60,000), small towns, and villages in which an estimated 6.5 million Canadians live.

Except in very special circumstances, the maximum capital available to any one BDC is $1.55 million. However, once transferred, the money remains in the hands of the community, and community members (within program guidelines) make the decisions regarding loans. Collectively, these BDCs have the potential for receiving and exercising control over $333 million in loans.

Mike Lewis, Westcoast Development Group, "Claiming Capital for Our Communities," in *Making Waves* (Vol 4., No. 2, May 1993).

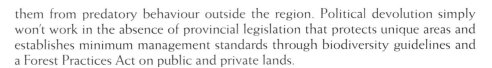
them from predatory behaviour outside the region. Political devolution simply won't work in the absence of provincial legislation that protects unique areas and establishes minimum management standards through biodiversity guidelines and a Forest Practices Act on public and private lands.

Toward a community economy

Devolution, both political and economical, is the key to ecological and economic sustainability in the competitive new global market. In particular, it is essential that our communities have sufficient ownership and control of their forests that they can choose the mix of uses they want. The provincial government can aid this devolution, and ensure that it is implemented in an orderly, fair way. If our present economy is subsidized by the unsustainable exploitation of our environment and communities, the jurisdiction that restructures itself to ensure sustainability can be unique in having dispensed with subsidies. It can, in other words, set the standard for future competitiveness that others must meet, a standard that reflects not just a narrow competitive advantage in one sector, but a cumulative advantage in the way in which the political and economic fabric is woven.

In the environmental community, the phrase "sustainable development" has long been the butt of a very telling throwaway line: "They got the noun, and we got the adjective." In contrast, moving to the value economy does not require minor alterations but creating something new after phasing out policies and programs that sap communities and natural environments of their health. This is the function of the community-based economic strategy that Don McMillan, a community economic development officer, talks about. Like any modern

Balanced trade

No policy prescription commands greater consensus among economists than that of free trade based on international specialization according to comparative advantage. Free Trade has long been presumed good unless proved otherwise....

Yet that presumption should be reversed. The default position should favor domestic production for domestic markets. When convenient, balanced international trade should be used, but it should not be allowed to govern a country's affairs at the risk of environmental and social disaster....

This wiser course was well expressed in the overlooked words of John Maynard Keynes: "I sympathize, therefore, with those who would minimize, rather than those who would maximize, economic entanglement between nations. Ideas, art, hospitality, travel—these are the things which should of their nature be international. But let goods be home spun whenever it is reasonably and conveniently possible; and above all, let finance be primarily national."

Economists and environmentalists are sometimes represented as being,

respectively, for and against free trade, but that polarization does the argument a disservice. Rather the real debate is over what kinds of regulations are to be instituted and what goals are legitimate. The free traders seek to maximize profits and production without regard for considerations that represent hidden social costs. They argue that when growth has made people wealthy enough, they will have the funds to clean up the damage done by growth. Conversely, environmentalists and some economists, myself among them, suspect that growth is increasing faster than benefits from production—thereby making us poorer, not richer....

Economists rightly urge nations to follow a domestic program of internalizing costs into prices. They also wrongly urge nations to trade freely with other countries that do not internalize their costs (and consequently have lower prices). If a nation tries to follow both those policies, the conflict is clear: free competition between different cost-internalizing regimes is utterly unfair.

International trade increases competition, and competition reduces costs. But competition can reduce costs in two ways: by increasing efficiency or by

lowering standards. A firm can save money by lowering its standards for pollution control, worker safety, wages, health care, and so on—all choices that externalize some of its costs. Profit maximizing firms in competition always have an incentive to externalize their costs to the degree that they can get away with it....

The most practical solution is to permit nations that internalize costs to levy compensating tariffs on trade with nations that do not. "Protectionism"— shielding an inefficient industry against more efficient foreign competitors—is a dirty word among economists. That is very different, however, from protecting an efficient national policy of full-cost pricing from standards-lowering international competition.

Such tariffs are also not without precedent. Free traders generally praise the fairness of "anti-dumping" tariffs that discourage countries from trading in goods at prices below their production costs. The only real difference is the decision to include the costs of environmental damage and community welfare in that reckoning.

Herman Daly, "The Perils of Free Trade," in *Scientific American* (November 1993).

industrial strategy, it takes a great deal of vision and commitment.

At its most fundamental level, developing sustainability will entail a broad transfer of tenure rights from corporate and Crown control to individual and local community ownership. A range of opportunities exists here, from the Swedish woodlot model, to the American experience with community land trusts and community forests, to Native land title. Such shifts in property rights would provoke an explosion in hitherto unseen job-intensive, low-technology, high-service, rural and community-based economic activity.

Backing this up would be community-based small business development. Again, precedents on the margins of government policy aren't hard to find, such as the federal government's popular and successful Community Futures program. At issue here, however, is not choosing one program or another but persuading government to stop marginalizing, even discriminating against small businesses, and start making them the cornerstone of a new strategy of community-based development. Whether it is the complex regulations and onerous loads of paperwork that drain an entrepreneur's energy from the tasks at hand, the bureaucratic predilection for large-scale technologies and corporations as in the federal government's multi-billion-dollar Western Economic Diversification Program, or an inattention to the special capital needs of small businesses, government is a major obstacle to small business success. The precarious situation of BC's emergent remanufacturing sector is a perfect example of this problem.

As Prince Rupert's Mike Tarr, Chairman of BC Central Credit Union, put it: "Government could do an awful lot towards turning around the climate for small business in the province and not have to get involved in massive planning exercises. But the bureaucracy has gotten out of control, and grass-roots intelligence is no longer a major factor."

Government attitudes are not the only obstacle. Witness the attitudes of the other partners in our modern-day corporatism, big labour and big business. Instead of hitching their fortunes to a burning-out corporate star, union leaders should be working hard to champion causes that put people to work. There may be tradeoffs involved—lower rates of pay, different types of work, mill-specific rather than industry-wide contract agreements. But the potential gain is job

Possibilities to finance small, ecologically sound businesses abound. Here, Rick Walton's S.A.W. Millwork Inc. uses a Wood-Mizer portable sawmill which can be purchased new for about $30,000. With trees selectively logged from a second-growth forest near Horn Lake, north of Qualicum, Walton cuts lumber that is then used to make timber frame buildings. Walton's profitable company is one of a growing number of small sawmilling ventures operating in BC. Chip Vinai photo.

BC is already producing a host of valuable wood products like the spindles and other products seen here. But much more can be produced when the province starts to collect more money from companies cutting old-growth. With more money paid up front, there is greater incentive to get more from the raw product. BC Wood Specialties Group Association photo.

Below: The proliferation of ecologos worldwide foretells a rise in market pressures for alternative forest practices.

security and job satisfaction, conditions sorely lacking in today's volume economy. Union members displaced from jobs in volume-driven mills might be the first to lay claim to new woodlots or work in community forests. Similarly, mill workers could be supported in setting up new sawmill co-operatives and small manufacturing businesses, as they have done in the past on an ad hoc basis to save a mill or a plant from being abandoned in the restructuring plans of a major company. In this way, unions could help facilitate changes that value labour more than capital, that emphasize community and worker health over corporate profit. Indeed, were the union movement forward-looking, facilitating the transition from corporate dependence to co-operative community independence would become its major objective. This would set the context for a wholesale shift in the economic landscape toward a new economy of genuine productivity. Laura Tyson, Chairperson of US President Bill Clinton's Council of Economic Advisors, has decisively proven in study after study that the single key to "productive investment" is worker involvement, especially worker ownership.

Existing government programs in retraining and "industrial adjustment" would then be reoriented to help achieve this integrated objective. As it is, by ignoring the social dimensions of unemployment, large quantities of money are wasted attempting to turn unemployed labourers who can barely read into high-tech computer operators, or trying to move people out of hard-hit communities when their passions tell them to stay put and help their neighbours survive.

And, of course, there is the need for money. But as we have seen, the possibilities abound. Again, the provincial government's role is central because capital is averse to the risks involved in supporting the restructuring needed. Like small business development and labour adjustment, this component of our industrial strategy demands a package of financial initiatives. Its foundation is not governments throwing money at communities, but redirecting the returns of resource ownership and manufacturing back to communities through private log markets and locally collected resource taxes. The provincial government can further enhance this process by directing existing institutions, especially credit unions and pension funds, to invest in community enterprises with the support of government-backed loan guarantees and risk-sharing arrangements. Billions of dollars are available from redirecting existing resources without a dollar of new public money being spent.

The fine details of an economic strategy, like those of political devolution, are many and complicated. Implementing them will not be easy. But we will undertake the task with pleasure if we understand, as Jim Smith, Herman Hans, Gian Sandhu and Loni Parker do, the possibilities that await us when we make that commitment.

CHAPTER TEN

REINVENTING B.C.

A S THE MASSIVE, HIGHLY ORCHESTRATED PROTESTS AGAINST the Commission on Resources and Environment attest, many people would have us believe that all land-use disputes in British Columbia centre on a choice between high-paying jobs in the forest industry and protection of some of the last wild places left. For years, industry-financed Share groups and other organizations such as the Forest Alliance of BC have cultivated support in resource-dependent communities around BC, by keeping the debate over the future of the forest industry narrowly focussed and polarized along these lines. Their strategy has been wildly successful. Loggers and mill workers are, indeed, frightened about their future. And many are quick to blame their woes on urban environmentalists. Just as H.R. MacMillan complained about provincial forest bureaucrats half a century ago, now Gerry Furney, the mayor of Port McNeill, damns these people who "don't know what it's like to get rain in their lunch buckets."

When CORE released its recommendations for Vancouver Island in a report calling for a nominal increase (less than 3 percent) in protected areas on the island, the reaction was swift and loud. Thousands of jobs were sure to be lost, Furney and others told receptive loggers and mill workers. "Twelve percent and no more," became the rallying cry, as forest industry workers demanded Premier Mike Harcourt stick to his government's stated policy of protecting 12 percent of BC in parks and wilderness while leaving the rest of the land base open to industrial development. Given the dynamics of the volume-driven economy, it is understandable why many, many forest industry workers are frightened today. In their eyes, anything that disrupts the flow of logs to the mills spells trouble. And in the high-profile activities of environmental protesters, they see the source of that trouble personified. So the loggers take to the streets in their own protests. And in the twenty-second sound bites that pass for news in the next day's press and radio accounts, loggers warn about the certain loss of high-paying jobs, while environmentalists talk about the certain loss of irreplaceable wilderness.

To get beyond this stalemate requires substantive changes to the way we conduct business in BC. This was something CORE Commissioner Stephen Owen realized as he and others toured Vancouver Island in the months leading up to their report. Everywhere they went, people were entrenched in old positions. Scepticism ran high, with many in the environmental and labour communities refusing to have anything to do with the process. In releasing its report, CORE tried to move beyond simply defining which areas should be protected and which areas left open for development by recommending an

Opposite:
Temperate rain forest on the West Coast of Vancouver Island. Alan Etkin photo.
Insets, left to right:
Tree planter. Myron Kozak photo.
Small sawmiller. Myron Kozak photo.
Boatbuilder. Alan Etkin photo.

Economic Transition Strategy for Vancouver Island. "As a matter of equity and in order to reconcile environmental with economic and social sustainability, a transition strategy is essential to respond to the needs of those communities and individuals who will be affected by implementation of this Plan," CORE reported.

The report went on to recommend that this plan should focus on "generating new jobs in forestry where the skills, experience and resource potentials exist." And it said a fundamental goal of the plan should be to generate more employment by "extending the range of products produced from the resources." The Commission said the industry needed to make more product from an available but ever-shrinking supply of natural resources—in short, to shift from a volume-driven to a value-added approach. These were telling observations. But they were given short shrift in the report. Indeed, of the 260 pages of CORE's recommendations for Vancouver Island, a scant 10 pages at the back of the text were devoted to articulating a new vision for our forest industry. Still, it was an attempt to focus public attention on the wider issues at stake in our struggle to preserve wilderness and maintain a healthy forest industry. And it's something that desperately needs to be discussed now.

In the absence of a new economic strategy, debates over the future of BC's forests will remain mired in unhealthy, unproductive skirmishes over one watershed or another. To government will fall the dubious honour of deciding which valleys are logged and which aren't. Or, worse yet, which parts of valleys will be logged and which spared. That approach, as the historic protests in Clayoquot in the spring and summer of 1993 show, leaves everybody unhappy. Intact ecosystems end up being fragmented, to the dismay of environmental activists, while the supply of wood to distant mills shrinks, putting further pressure on workers already hard-hit in the volume economy.

It is time that we moved beyond the divisive debates over specific wilderness valleys and how they affect various mills, to an honest discussion of our goals and how they mesh or clash with today's economy. In BC, the challenges that we confront are specific to our forest-dependent economy; nevertheless the problem is widely shared by an industrialized world overshooting its ecological and economic base. In Canada, whether it is the depleted or dwindling East or West Coast fisheries, the debt-leveraged and mega-project-dependent energy industry in Ontario, the struggling Prairie farmers, or gas-guzzling and garbage-exporting cities, a pattern of costly and inefficient overextension is omnipresent. Any serious attempt to get past our present morass must start with the embrace of a larger change.

In British Columbia, too, we are overextended, and maintaining the status quo means an impoverished future. The annual cut is falling, and will continue to do so. Must we simply fight over the scraps where everyone loses, or can we shift the entire debate to a new vision where everyone can win? Making this shift is the promise of Forestopia.

In this book, we have been critical of the volume economy—big companies that control the land base, big governments that allow massive overcutting, big volumes of timber flowing away for someone else's benefit, a big inheritance of old-growth diamonds that is being smashed to bits and squandered. The Forest Renewal Act addresses some aspects of the problem, but fails to challenge the corporatism and tragic waste at its roots. A broader strategy of alternative economic development such as we propose may seem radical, but the changes in the institutional landscape that we suggest are not.

On the one hand, we begin with an invigorated market, hardly an unsettling suggestion for a free-enterprise society. Today, the Big has become the enemy of the Good, with most economic prescriptions focussing on the needs of

Waddington Channel on the north coast of BC. Al Harvey photo.

large integrated companies. But if a community wants stable employment, it must have many small businesses, not one big one. If a community's objective is to have a healthy resource base, it must have many local forest stewards that can nurture the landscape in perpetuity, not distant shareholders that can cut and run. If a community's objective is to escape its dependence on fickle commodity-driven export markets, it must have economic diversi-fication and flexible businesses that can serve local and long-distance markets together.

On the other hand, unlike the Forest Renewal Act, we do not advocate a return to the heavy-handed government of the past. Economic growth in both the office towers of Vancouver and the government coffers of Victoria is subsidized by the erosion of local environments and local commun-ities. Ever anxious to placate the powers that be, governments have been mired in indecision, in half-truths and in half-measures. Half-measures will not work any more; only the transition to a new value economy, with a devolution to economic diversity and community revitalization, can solve our woes. In this book, just as we are pro-market (but envision a different sort of market), so too we may be seen as anti-government, yet see a critical role for govern-ment.

And let us make no mistake about it—the opportunities that await us if we can begin that transition are huge. If we merge the job benefits from developing an industry around pruning and thinning our second-growth forests, from setting aside our heritage old-growth for new tourism and amenities-based industries, from encouraging selection logging in thousands of new woodlots and community forests, from implementing and even going beyond the recommendations of the Evans report on remanufacturing, from harnessing the power of the market so as to return local capital to local communities, from seeking out a broad new investment strategy for our local capital, then we are talking not about a few, but about tens upon tens of thousands of new jobs, jobs that will last, jobs that are healthy, jobs that will make peace in the province.

To make this happen, the resources of a provincial government that are now dedicated to propping up the old forest economy must be redirected into a small business and community-based transition. And this must happen now. A significant base of biodiversity and sheer SuperNatural beauty could be preserved in this wonderful land that we all call home, at the same time as the foundation is laid for a new economic vitality. But to move past the old unsustainable economics of corporate and bureaucratic growth into a new value-based economy rooted in territorial health, we must also move from an old to a new politics.

In many small ways, the transition is already underway—and working. People like Jim Smith are quietly working away in the woods, proving every day that it is possible to log in more environmentally responsible ways than today's often destructive clearcutting. In the mills we've seen how people like Gian Sandhu are creating jobs by processing partly manufactured lumber into high-value wood components. In our sadly neglected second-growth forests we've seen how people like Mike Steeves are creating jobs logging trees that the major forest companies show little interest in. In Nanaimo we've seen how Don McMillan, a local economic development officer, worked with the local credit union to put more people back to work in the vitally important small business sector. It is time for these inspiring leaders and many others to come forward into a new movement and a new politics that demands innovation and co-operation from environmentalists and loggers alike, from small businesses and progressive labour leaders, from Natives and local governments.

British Columbia at the close of the twentieth century is on the verge of catastrophe or a new beginning. With the demonstrations and the shrill attacks, we can choose economic surrender; or we can take stock of our dimming present but potentially bright future, and rebuild. British Columbia still has the luxury of being able to reinvent its economics and its politics. If we take this opportunity, we can make peace and prosperity at home. The world is watching.

Print

Bateman, Robert. Open letter to CBC radio. 1993.

Best, Michael. *The New Competition: Institutions of Industrial Restructuring.* Cambridge MA: Harvard University Press, 1991.

British Columbia. *British Columbia's Forest Renewal Plan.* April, 1994.

British Columbia. Commission on Resources and Environment. Socio-Economic Information binder, 1993.

British Columbia. Forest Resources Commission. *Community Employment Dependencies.* 1992.

British Columbia. Forest Resources Commission. *The Future of Our Forests.* 1991.

British Columbia. Forest Resources Commission. Vancouver Island Land Use Plan. 1994.

British Columbia. Legislative Assembly. *Official Report of Debates.* Vol. 10, No. 19, June 3, 1993.

British Columbia. Ministry of Environment, Lands and Parks. "Managing Wildlife to 2001: A Discussion Paper." 1991.

British Columbia. Ministry of Forests. *Ecosystems of British Columbia.* 1991.

British Columbia. Ministry of Forests. *Towards an Old-Growth Strategy.* 1992.

British Columbia. Ministry of Regional and Economic Development. *Small Business in British Columbia 1979–1989: A Decade of Change.* 1990.

British Columbia. Ministry of Regional and Economic Development. *Strengthening Small Business in the 90s.* 1990.

British Columbia. Select Standing Committee on Forest and Lands. *Forest Act:* Part 12 (Log Exports) and *The Vancouver Log Market.* 1990 and 1991.

British Columbia. Select Standing Committee on Forests, Energy, Mines and Petroleum Resources. *Lumber Remanufacturing in British Columbia: First Report.* 1993.

British Columbia. Select Standing Committee on Forests, Energy, Mines and Petroleum Resources. *Report of Proceedings.* No. 15, 1993.

British Columbia. Select Standing Committee on Forests, Energy, Mines and Petroleum Resources. *Report of Proceedings.* No. 18, 1993.

Business Council of British Columbia. Comments on the Proposed Forest Practices Code. December 1993.

Canada. Forest Sector Advisory Council. *Canada's Forest Industry: A Strategy for Growth.* July 1992.

Canada. Ministry of Employment and Immigration, Statistics Canada. *Skill Shifts in our Economy: A Decade in the Life of British Columbia.* Prepared by R. Kunin and J. Knauf. 1992.

Carlson, Gordon, quoted in *Report of Proceedings of the Select Standing Committee on Forests, Energy, Mines and Petroleum Resources.* Issue 8, Ladysmith, January 12, 1993.

CCG Consulting Group Ltd. *Timber and Log Markets for the Forest Resources of British Columbia* (Study conducted for BC Forest Resources Commission). 1992.

Center for Policy Alternatives. "Background Paper on Economically Targeted Investments." Washington DC, 1993.

Coalition of Community Development Finance Institutions. *CDFIs: Key Tools for Rebuilding Communities.* Yardley PA, January 1993.

Commission on Resources and Environment. *Vancouver Island Land Use Plan 1.* February 1994.

"Criteria for the Sustainable Development of Canada's Forests." Working paper prepared for the CSCE Seminar of Experts on the Sustainable Development of Temperate and Boreal Forests, Conference on Security and Co-operation in Europe. Montreal, September 27–October 1, 1993.

Cuthbert, John. Speech delivered at College of New Caledonia Logging Seminar. Reprinted in *BCEN Report,* December 1992.

Daly, Herman. "The Perils of Free Trade," in *Scientific American.* November 1993.

Davis, W. *Shadows in the Sun: Essays on the Spirit of Place.* Edmonton: Lone Pine Publishing, 1992.

Dellert, Lois. Letter to Ian Gill, CBC-TV. February 1991.

Drushka, Ken. *Stumped: The Forest Industry in Transition.* Vancouver: Douglas & McIntyre, 1985.

Drushka, Ken, et al, eds. *Touch Wood: BC Forests at the Crossroads.* Madeira Park BC: Harbour Publishing Ltd., 1993.

Ecotrust and Conservation International. "Coastal Temperate Rain Forests: Ecological Characteristics, Status and Distribution Worldwide." Occasional Paper Series No. 1, Abstract, 1992.

Evans, Corky, speech in the BC Legislative Assembly. *Hansard.* Vol. 10, No. 19, June 3, 1993.

Fletcher Challenge Canada Ltd., *Newsline.* 1993.

Forest Perspectives, Portland OR. Vol. 3, Issue 3, Autumn 1993.

Forestry Canada. *The State of Forestry in Canada: 1990 Report to Parliament.* 1991.

Forest Summit. *Rising to the Challenge.* 1992.

Forintek Canada Corp. and Wayne B. Trusty & Associates Ltd. "Forintek's Western Laboratory: Building in Wood to Meet Environmental Objectives." 1991.

Fox, Irving K. "Canada–United States Trade in Forest Products: Issues and Uncertainties," in *Emerging Issues in Forest Policy,* ed. Peter N. Nemetz. Vancouver BC: UBC Press, 1992.

Franklin, Jerry. "Old-Growth Forests and the New Forestry," in "Forests Wild and Managed: Differences and Consequences." Symposium notes, University of British Columbia, January 19–20, 1990.

Gadgil, M. and R. Guha. *This Fissured Land: An Ecological History of India.* Berkeley CA: University of California Press, 1992.

Gilfillan, B. D. et al. *Report of a Forestry Mission to Scandinavia.* Report 156. Victoria BC: Forest Resources Development Agreement, 1990.

Haley, David. *Seminar proceedings of Determining Timber Supply & Allowable Cuts in BC.* Vancouver: UBC, March 1993.

Hawken, Paul. *The Ecology of Commerce.* New York: HarperCollins, 1993.

Hopwood, Doug. "Principles and Practices of New Forestry: A Guide for British Columbians." Ministry of Forests, Land Management Report Number 71, 1991.

Hyslop, R. J. & Associates Ltd. *Report to Province of British Columbia, Ministry of Forests, Economics and Trade Branch, Ministry of Economic Development, Small Business and Trade, Victoria, BC on Coastal Softwood Plywood.* 1992

Johnston, Kirk. *Beyond Polarization: Emerging Strategies for Reconciling Community and the Environment.* Seattle WA: University of Washington, Northwest Policy Center, 1993.

Jones, Trevor. Critique of methods the BC Government uses to assess socio-economic implications of forestry/conservation strategies. Consultant's report, January 1994.

Jones, Trevor and François Depey, "Inventory of Watersheds in the Southern Interior of BC." Unpublished paper, 1991.

Lewis, Kaaren, Andy MacKinnon and Dennis Hamilton. "Protected Areas Planning." Paper presented to Habitat Futures Conference: Expanding Horizons on Forest Ecosystem Management. Vernon BC, October 21, 1992.

Lewis, Mike. "Claiming Capital for Our Communities," in *Making Waves.* Vol 4., No. 2, May 1993.

Lidstone, D. "Local Communities and the Future of Forest Resources." Prepared for Annual Meeting, Association of Kootenay Boundary Municipalities, Radium Hot Springs. 1993.

Luckert, M. K. and D. Haley. "Canadian Forest Tenures and the Silvicultural Investment Behaviour of Rational Firms," in *Canadian Journal of Forest Research.* Vol. 23, No. 6, 1993.

Ludwig, Donald, Ray Hilborn and Carl Walters. "Uncertainty, Resource Exploitation, and Conservation: Lessons from History," in *Science.* No. 260, 1993.

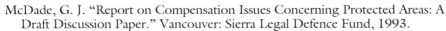

McDade, G. J. "Report on Compensation Issues Concerning Protected Areas: A Draft Discussion Paper." Vancouver: Sierra Legal Defence Fund, 1993.

MacMillan Bloedel Ltd. "Adding Value to the Forest," in *Forest Perspectives*. December 1991.

MacMillan Bloedel Ltd. *Annual Statutory Report*. 1992.

Marchak, M. Patricia. "Global Markets in Forest Products: Sociological Impacts on Kyoto Prefecture and British Columbia Interior Forest Regions." Paper prepared for *Journal of Business Administration*, special edition on forestry management policy. 1989.

Markvoort, J. W. "Review of Timber and Log Markets" (Background report prepared for the British Columbia Forest Resources Commission). 1992.

Mascall, Michael. *Public Investment by Governments in the BC Forest Industry 1991/92*. Quathiaski Cove BC: Mascall & Associates, March 1994.

M'Gonigle, Michael. "Developing Sustainability: A Native/Environmentalist Prescription for Third-Level Government," in *BC Studies*. Vol. 84.

Moore, K. *Coastal Watersheds: An Inventory of Watersheds in the Coastal Temperate Forests of British Columbia*. Earthlife Canada Foundation and Ecotrust/Conservation International: 1991.

Nawitka Resource Consultants. *Increasing Utilization Level of British Columbia's Timber Harvest*. Report 121. Victoria BC: Forest Resource Development Agreement, 1990.

North Cariboo Community Futures. *Region in Transition: An Economic Profile and Development Strategy for the North Cariboo Region of BC*. 1988.

Northwest Policy Center. *Improving the Vitality of Oregon's Secondary Wood Products Sector*. Report for the Oregon Interim Legislative Committee on Forest Policy. Seattle WA: University of Washington, 1990.

Ontario. Ministry of Municipal Affairs. "Community Economic Development Financing Mechanisms." Discussion paper, June 1993.

Pine, Jim, quoted in *Report of Proceedings of the Select Standing Committee on Forests, Energy, Mines and Petroleum Resources*. Issue 7, Victoria, January 11, 1993.

Pulp, Paper and Woodworkers of Canada. *Jobs, Trees & Us: The PPWC's Forest Policy*. 1993.

Rees, William E. "The Ecology of Sustainable Development," in *The Ecologist*. Vol. 20, No. 1, 1990.

Rewalkowski, Larry, quoted in *Report of Proceedings of the Select Standing Committee on Forests, Energy, Mines and Petroleum Resources*. Issue 8, Ladysmith, January 12, 1993.

Sale, Kirkpatrick. *Dwellers in the Land: The Bioregional Vision*. San Francisco: Sierra Club Books, 1985.

Sanders, Peter. Paper presented as part of a panel discussion "Tenure and the Future". Reprinted in *Truck Logger*, February–March 1990.

Sayegh, Jacques. "Venture Capital Redefined," in *Canadian Banker*. Vol. 99, No. 3, May–June 1992.

Schwindt, Richard. *Report of the Royal Commission of Inquiry into Compensation for the Taking of Resource Interests*. 1993.

Science Council of British Columbia. *Forestry Research and Development in British Columbia: A Vision for the Future*. October 1989.

Slocan Valley Community Forest Management Project. *Final Report*, 2nd ed. Winlaw BC, 1976.

Sommers, P. and H. Birss. *Improving the Vitality of the Secondary Wood Products Sector in Oregon* (Final report for the Oregon Interim Legislative Committee on Forest Products Policy). Seattle: Northwest Policy Centre, Institute for Public Policy and Management, University of Washington, 1990.

Sterling Wood Group. *Analysis of Changes in Timber Values due to Silviculture Treatments Under the Forest Resource Development Agreement*. Report 41. Victoria BC: Forest Resources Development Agreement, 1988.

Travers, O. R. (Ray). "History of Logging and Sustained Yield in BC, 1911–90," in *Forest Planning Canada*. Vol. 8, No. 1, January–February 1992.

Tripp, D. et al. *The Application and Effectiveness of the Coastal Fisheries Forestry Guidelines in Selected Cut Blocks on Vancouver Island*. British Columbia, Ministry of Environment, Lands and Parks: 1992.

Truck Loggers' Association. "BC's Forests: A Vision for Tomorrow." Working papers, 1990.

Truck Loggers' Association. "The State of the Resource," in *Forest Planning Canada*. Vol. 7, No. 2, 1991.

Union of British Columbia Municipalities. *Local Government and the Constitutions*. Richmond BC, 1991.

Union of Concerned Scientists. "World Scientists' Warning to Humanity." 1993.

United States. Department of Commerce. *Preliminary Affirmative Countervailing Duty Determination: Certain Softwood Lumber Products from Canada*. International Trade Administration, March 1992.

United States. Forest Service. Technical report, cited in Natural Resource Defense Council Memorandum "Summary of Issues Related to the Recent California Spotted Owl Decision." San Francisco, January 21, 1993.

Vancouver *Sun*, April 17, 1993, July 17, 1993, March 22, 1994.

Verchere, David, quoted in *Report of Proceedings of the Select Standing Committee on Forests, Energy, Mines and Petroleum Resources*. Issue 15, Williams Lake, January 25, 1993.

Village of Hazelton. *Framework for Watershed Stewardship* Village of Hazelton BC, 1991.

Walmsley, M. et al. *Evaluation of Soil Degradation as a Factor Affecting Forest Productivity in British Columbia—A Problem Analysis*. Report 038. Victoria BC: Forest Resources Development Agreement, 1988.

Western Wood Products Forum. *Human Resources in the British Columbia Wood Products Industry*. 1993.

Wilkinson, John. *Undeveloped Watersheds on Vancouver Island Larger than 1000 Hectares*. Ministry of Forests, Recreation Branch, 1992:3, 1990.

Wismer, S. "Sustainable Development and Urban Life," in William Rees, *Defining Sustainable Development*. CHS Research Bulletin, University of British Columbia Centre for Human Settlements, 1989.

Wood, R. S. "An Analysis of the Forest Industry Employment Situation in Port Alberni." Prepared for Mr. Douglas Kerley, Provincial Job Protection Commissioner. 1991.

Interviews

Harry Bains, third vice-president, IWA–Canada 1–217, Vancouver.
Jack Bakewell, retired professional forester, Vancouver.
Hank Bonthuis, former MacMillan Bloedel Ltd. employee.
Tom Bradley, forest technician, Silva Ecosystem Consultants.
Gerry Bracewell, Chilcotin wilderness lodge operator.
Mark Brett, Port Alberni sawmill employee.
Hank Cameron, forest technician, Cherryville.
David Cohen, professor of forestry, Faculty of Forestry, University of British Columbia.
Energy and Paperworkers Union of Canada.
Grant Copeland, economic consultant, New Denver.
Ken Drushka, author, Vancouver.
Roger Ennis, forest industry analyst, B.C. Trade, Vancouver.
Corky Evans, NDP MLA for Nelson-Creston.
Ross Gentleman, Ministry of Finance Financial Institutions Commission (FICOM), and co-founder of CCEC Credit Union.
Rod Gould, horse logger, Greenwood.
Trevor Goward, lichenologist, University of B.C.
David Haley, forest economist, Faculty of Forestry, University of B.C.
Herman Hans, director, Real Market Loggers Association, Prince Rupert.
Mollie Harrington, former business development officer, Quesnel.

Colin Harte, Indpendent Lumber Remanufacturers Association, Vancouver.
Greg Jadrzyk, vice-president, Council of Forest Industries, Prince George.
Jean Jeanrenaud, forests campaigner, Worldwide Fund for Nature, London, England.
Gilbert King, displaced Williams Lake sawmill worker.
Colleen McCrory, Chairperson, Valhalla Wilderness Society.
Kevin McElvey, Community Futures, Quesnel.
Bill McIntosh, woodlot owner, Vanderhoof.
Andy MacKinnon, Ministry of Forests, Victoria.
Don McMillan, general manager, Central Island Community Development Society, Nanaimo.
Mike Major, former log scaler and consultant, Victoria.
Francis Maltby, environmental campaigner, Revelstoke.
Charles Merriam, independent sawmiller, Cherryville.
Graham Morgan, unemployed sawmill worker, Gitwangak Reserve.
Dave Neads, Chilcotin environmental campaigner.
Loni Parker, director, Revelstoke Community Forest Corporation.
Don Ryan, spokesman for the Gitksan and Wet'suwet'en Hereditary Chiefs.
Gian Sandhu, president, Jackpine Forest Products, Williams Lake.
Wayne Sawchuk, Chetwynd logger, turned environmental campaigner.
Gerry Sillers, partner, B.W. Creative Wood Industries Ltd., Maple Ridge.
Sile Simpson, Tofino bed and breakfast manager.
Jim Smith, Ministry of Forests, Vernon.
Mike Steeves, president, Texada Logging, Victoria.
Dave Steinhauer, second vice-president, IWA–Canada, Local 1–85.
Tom Strong, psychologist, regional mental health centre, Smithers.
Mike Tarr, Chairman, BC Central Credit Union.
Len Thiessen, independent sawmiller, Cherryville.
Ray Travers, forestry consultant, Victoria.
David White, part-time longshoreman, Stewart.
Keith Wyton, president, Sarita Furniture Ltd., Port Alberni.

Other Media

Commission on Resources and Environment. Public Meeting, Vancouver Island, 1993.
Kogawa, Joy. Presentation at Writers for Clayoquot Sound festival, Vancouver, 1993.
Narayanan, Hon. Shri K. R. Inaugural address delivered at First Ministerial Conference on Forestry Forum for Developing Countries. New Delhi, India, September 1–3, 1993.
Sierra Club of Western Canada. Comments on the Forest Practices Code. December 1993.

Ainsworth Lumber, 73
Apsey, Mike, 47
Armleder, Harold, 33–34
Bains, Harry, 40
Bakewell, Jack, 64–66
BC Building Corporation, 91
BC Door Co. Ltd., 83
BC Science Council, 60
biodiversity, 33–37, 47, 54
Biport Forest Products, 73
Bonthuis, Hank, 9–10
Bowron Lakes, 30
Bracewell, Gerry, 24–25
Bradley, Tom, 32
"Brazil of the North," 29, 47
Brett, Mark, 11, 15, 55
Bruce, Graham, 77
Business Development Centres, 101
B.W. Creative Wood Industries Ltd., 89
Cameron, Hank, 59
Campbell River, 42
Canadian Forest Products Ltd., 45; Canfor Specialty, 86
Canadian Wood Council, 91
Cariboo Lumber Manufacturers' Association, 83
Carlson, Gordon, 85
Carnaby sawmill, 19, 44
Cascade Cedar Products Ltd., 100
Castlegar, 53
Celgar Pulp, 53, 73
Central Island Community Development Society (CICDS), 80–81
Chemainus, 22
Cherryville, 59–60, 68, 75, 77, 88
Chetwynd, 31
Chilcotin, 20, 24–25
Clayoquot Sound, 9, 10–11, 12–13, 14, 16, 25, 45, 92–93, 98, 101; see also coastal temperate rain forests
Clinton, 26
coastal temperate rain forests, 19, 30, 54, 107
Cohen, David, 44
Cold Creek, 35
Collins Pine, 68
Columbia River basin, 100
Commission on Resources and Environment (CORE), 12–13, 14, 45, 99, 100, 107–108; see also Owen, Stephen

communities, resource-dependent; see resource-dependent communities
community control, 20, 21, 24–25, 54–57, 80–81, 98–105
community economic development, 15, 17, 55–57, 98–105; in Ontario, 81
Community Futures program, 21, 80–81, 101, 103
Copeland, Grant, 53
corporate concentration, 25, 44, 46, 95, 96–98
Council of Forest Industries of BC (COFI), 14, 47, 73, 76, 77, 85, 101
credit unions, 79–80, 80–81, 103
Davis, Wade, 29–30
Downie St. Sawmill, 100
Doyle, RCMP St. Sgt Len, 11
Drushka, Ken, 46, 62, 97
East Ootsa, 37
employment and unemployment, capital-to-labour shift, 55–56; dependence on forestry, 44–45; jobs per volume of wood, 22, 41, 83–93; layoffs and job losses, 9–13, 14, 22, 23–24, 26–27, 40–41, 44, 107, 108; social costs of unemployment, 19–20, 26–27, 56
Ennis, Roger, 92
Escalante, 29
Evans, Corky, 66, 83–93
export sales of BC wood, 39–47
Finland, forestry in, 61, 64, 65
Fletcher Challenge Canada Ltd., 45, 63, 95, 97, 98
Forest Alliance of BC, 29, 47
Forest Renewal Act (1994), 14, 15, 41, 60, 61, 74, 75, 85, 108, 109
Forest Resource Development Agreement, 62
Forest Resources Commission (FRC), 22, 31, 78, 93
Forest Sector Advisory Council, 23
Forests Summit '92, 46
Forintek, 91, 92
Fort Nelson, 31
Free Trade Agreement, 40, 102
Gitksan, 26–27
Gitwangak, 19–20, 27, 76
Gould, Rod, 66–67

government; *see* Harcourt, Mike; Ministry of Economic Development; Ministry of Forests; Ministry of Small Business, Tourism and Culture; Select Standing Committee on Forests, Energy, Mines and Petroleum Resources; Small Business Forest Enterprise Program

Goward, Trevor, 34

Grano Creek, 30–31

Greenpeace, 12, 29

Haley, David, 22, 32, 64

Hans, Herman, 43–44, 71–72

Harcourt, Premier Mike, 9, 12–13, 14; see also Forest Renewal Act

Harrington, Mollie, 21, 26

Harte, Colin, 87

Hinton, Alberta, 13

Horn Lake, 103

horse logging, 59–60, 66–67

Houston Forest Products, 11

Husband, Vicky, 23–24

Independent Lumber Remanufacturers' Association (ILRA), 87

Independent Timber Marketing Association, 78

International Forest Products Ltd. (Interfor), 71, 97

International Woodworkers of America (IWA), 14, 21, 22, 23, 24, 29, 40, 45, 47, 85, 86

investment in BC, 45–46

Jackpine Forest Products, 77–78, 88–89; *see also* Sandhu, Gian

Jadrzyk, Greg, 91

Japan, forestry in, 66

Jeanrenaud, Jean, 47–48

Jones, Kenneth, 83

Kaien Consumers Credit Union, 79–80

Kamloops, 79, 90

Kennedy, Jymm, 23

Keremeos, 51

King, Gilbert, 21

Kitlope River, 95

Kitselas band, 55, 71

Kozek Sawmills Ltd., 100

Lake Cowichan, 62

Lange, Karl, 83

Larrivee, Jean (Larrivee Guitars), 88

layoffs; *see* employment and unemployment

leave strips, 31

Liard River lowlands, 31

lichens, 33–34

Lignum Ltd., 77, 88, 89

Linde, Fred, 56

Long Run Sustained Yield, 31

Louisiana Pacific, 73

Lumby log market, 74–76, 79, 98

MacMillan, H. R., 107

MacMillan Bloedel Ltd., 10, 11, 12, 15, 22, 23, 25, 36–37, 41, 86, 87, 88

Major, Mike, 43, 76, 97–98

Maltby, Francis, 100

manufacturing networks, 90

market value for wood, 41–43, 71–81, 83–93, 98

Markvoort, Bill, 78–79

McCrory, Colleen, 29

McElvey, Kevin, 21–22

McIntosh, Bill, 68

McMillan, Don, 80–81, 102–103

Merriam, Charles, 77, 88

mill capacity, 23, 53

Miller, Dan, 95

Ministry of Economic Development, 73

Ministry of Forests, 19, 20, 31, 33, 46, 47, 66, 67, 74–75, 78, 80, 96, 101

Ministry of Small Business, Tourism and Culture, 95

Moore, Patrick, 29

Morgan, Graham, 19–20, 26, 55

Munro, Jack, 23, 29, 47

Nanaimo, 80–81

Nanaimo Credit Union, 80–81

Nass Valley, 31

Native British Columbians, 19–20, 26–27, 55, 71, 76, 97, 100, 101, 103

Neads, Dave, 20, 21

New Denver, 29

New Forest Economy, 16–17, 52–57, 71–81, 83–93

New Forestry, 63

North Central Plywood, 23

100 Mile House, 71

Ontario, community economic development in, 81

Orenda Pulp and Paper, 73

Owen, Stephen, 12, 107–108; *see also* Commission on Resources and Environment (CORE)
Pacific Forest Products, 63
Parker, Andrew, 46
Parker, Loni, 99–100
parklands, 36, 107
Pearse, Peter, 77
Petty, George, 23
Pope and Talbot Ltd., 30–31
Port Alberni, 9, 11, 23–24, 88, 92–93
Powell River, 65
Primex Forest Products Ltd., 62–63, 79
Prince George, 23, 91
Prince Rupert, 22, 71, 79–80, 91
profitability, 53
Pulp, Paper and Woodworkers Union, 23
Quesnel, 21–22, 26, 60, 90–91
rain forests; *see* coastal temperate rain forests
remanufacturing, 77, 78, 83–93
Repap International Inc., 23
resource-dependent communities, 15, 17, 21, 22, 24, 25–27, 39–40, 107; see also community control
Revelstoke, 99–100
Richmond, Claude, 47
Robinson, John, 52–53
Royal Canadian Mounted Police (RCMP), 11
Royal Commission on Timber Rights and Forest Policy (1976), 78
salmon; *see* wildlife
Sandhu, Gian, 77–78, 88–89, 90, 93
Sarita Furniture Ltd., 88
Sawchuk, Wayne, 31
S.A.W. Millwork Ltd., 103
Scientists, Union of Concerned, 13
Scoffield, Van, 83–84
Select Standing Committees, 66, 78, 86
Sierra Club, 24
Sillers, Gerry, 89
Silva Ecosystem Consultants, 32
silviculture, 23, 46, 54, 60–61, 65; thinning and pruning, 31, 62–63, 65–66
Simpson, Sile, 10–11, 15
Slocan Forest Products, 73
Slocan Valley Community Forest Management Project, 100–101
SLT Shortlog Thinning, 63

Small Business Forest Enterprise Program, 77–78, 85, 98
Smith, Jim, 56, 59–60, 75
Smithers, 26
social costs of unemployment, 19–20, 26–27, 56
South Moresby Park, 97
Steeves, Mike, 63, 64
Steinhauer, Dave, 24
Stewart, 25, 39
Strong, Tom, 26
stumpage fees, 14, 41, 72–81
sustainable development, 10, 31, 47, 52–53, 67, 102–103
Sustainable Development Research Institute, 52
sustained yield, 31, 32, 61
Sweden, forestry in, 61, 64, 65
Tackama Forest Products, 31
Tarr, Mike, 79–80, 91, 103
Task Force on Timber Disposal (1974), 77
tenure, 15, 43–44, 46, 59–69, 71–81, 83–93, 95–99, 103; *see also* tree farm licences
Terminal Forest Products Ltd., 40
Terrace, 55, 71
Texada Logging, 63
Thiessen, Len, 75
Timber West, 63
Tofino, 10, 93; *see also* Clayoquot Sound
tourism, 92–93
trade unions; *see* unions
Travers, O. R. (Ray), 41–43
Tree Farm Licences (TFLs), 19, 20, 41, 71, 99; *see also* tenure
Truck Loggers' Association, 60
Ucluelet, 9, 24; *see also* Clayoquot Sound
Uneeda Wood Products, 87
unemployment; *see* employment and unemployment
unions, 44, 46–47, 57, 66, 103–104; *see also* International Woodworkers of America (IWA); Pulp, Paper and Woodworkers Union
Valhalla Society, 53
value-added manufacturing, 23, 55, 57, 76, 83–93
value economy; *see* New Forest Economy
values, non-timber, 32, 91–92
Vancouver Forest Region, 90

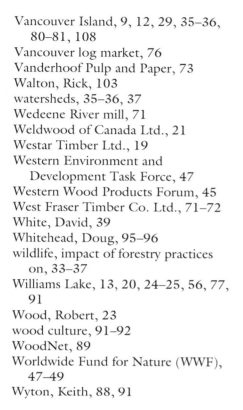

Vancouver Island, 9, 12, 29, 35–36,
    80–81, 108
Vancouver log market, 76
Vanderhoof Pulp and Paper, 73
Walton, Rick, 103
watersheds, 35–36, 37
Wedeene River mill, 71
Weldwood of Canada Ltd., 21
Westar Timber Ltd., 19
Western Environment and
    Development Task Force, 47
Western Wood Products Forum, 45
West Fraser Timber Co. Ltd., 71–72
White, David, 39
Whitehead, Doug, 95–96
wildlife, impact of forestry practices
    on, 33–37
Williams Lake, 13, 20, 24–25, 56, 77,
    91
Wood, Robert, 23
wood culture, 91–92
WoodNet, 89
Worldwide Fund for Nature (WWF),
    47–49
Wyton, Keith, 88, 91